Fragile like Glass:
The Underlying Vulnerabilities in the Financial System

Fragile like Glass:
The Underlying Vulnerabilities in the Financial System

Antonio Sánchez Serrano

Copyright © 2013 by Antonio Sánchez Serrano

All rights reserved. This book or any portion thereof may not be reproduced or used in any manner whatsoever without the express written permission of the publisher except for the use of brief quotations in a book review or scholarly journal.

The views expressed herein are solely those of the author, which is writing in his personal capacity, and they do not represent the views of his past or current employers. The content of this book is drawn from information publicly available and does never refer to any internal information he may have got from his past or current employers.

First Printing: December 2013

ISBN 978-1-291-59147-7

If you wish to contact the author, please write an e-mail to antsanch@gmail.com

Dedication

To my parents, Antonio and Maria,

To Andrea,

To Babätko,

Contents

Acknowledgements xi
Preface 1
Chapter 1: On the Brink of Financial Meltdown 5
   1.   The perfect storm 6
   2.   Once upon a time in America 11
   3.   Collateral damage in the EU 17
Chapter 2: Financial Markets for All 27
   4.   Rise of the machines 27
   5.   The need for speed 32
   6.   Money on a merry-go-round 37
   7.   But, tell me doctor, what does it mean to me? 40
Chapter 3: Conflict of Interest 44
   8.   The power of rating 45
   9.   Hunting fees 48
   10. Dangerous liaisons in accounting 50
Chapter 4: Capital Requirements 57
   11. The case for regulating banks 57
   12. The evolution of capital requirements 61
   13. Higher capital requirements or growth 64
Chapter 5: Policy Bites 70
   14. Does it need to be so complex? 70
   15. Liquidity and solvency: chicken and egg 74
   16. Purveyors of credit to the real economy 77
   17. The (not so) almighty monetary policy 81
   18. Regulators and supervisors reloaded 86
   19. Fewer names in the banking system 90
   20. Fields of data warehouses 96

Chapter 6: Of Incentives and Values 100
    21.   The stick, the carrot and rational decisions 100
    22.   I want it all, I want it now 104

Bibliography 109

Acknowledgements

I would like to thank Andrea for the continuous support and the very deep discussion about the content of this book. When clouds and doubts gathered over me, she always encouraged me to keep on writing. This book is certainly the result of her hard work as well.

The book reflects what I have learnt in the last five years, working with many colleagues, to whom I am also grateful. There is no point in writing their names here; I and they know who they are.

Antonio Sánchez Serrano

Preface

When first heard of some turmoil in the financial markets in the US, back in 2007, few could imagine that we were going to be still immersed in it six years later, with little hopes of having a significant improvement in the short-term. The fall of Lehman Brothers in September 2008 puzzled everybody and brought the financial system very close to collapse. Nonetheless, at that time, it was perceived as the beginning of the end, when it was just the trigger of more difficulties to come, as we have unfortunately discovered afterwards. Comparisons to the Great Recession, which were considered out of context at the beginning of the crisis, are now digested without problems by the public. The fall of Lehman was more than the fall of a bank, it also unmasked many externalities and imbalances which had been growing hidden in the financial markets and which made them more fragile, volatile and complex.

The pages hereinafter present my account of these interesting and challenging times, discussing as well the policy responses which are being put forward to repair our financial system, on the one hand, and to avoid similar episodes to happen again in the future, on the other. As already stated above, the financial crisis has unmasked many vulnerabilities and unaddressed issues which hamper the functioning and the ability of the financial system to effectively meet its core objective of financing the real economy. Some of these vulnerabilities and issues are being tackled by the regulatory and supervisory community as a reaction to the crisis, but some others are not the subject of any policy action. If we really want to leave this behind, the policy response to the crisis shall be comprehensive and cover all the participants in the financial markets. In other words, we would be giving a wrong response to the crisis if the only focus of regulatory and supervisory action is on capital requirements for banks.

It is indeed very difficult to find somebody who has not read any book about the financial crisis. Even so a new literary sub-genre seems to have emerged. From a privileged position, I have witnessed how the financial turmoil was born and spread. I have thus felt that I had something to add, my humble contribution, to what has been written so far. In doing so, I have tried to develop a text which is not too technical for the average reader but which, at the same time, goes deep into policy. I have refrained from doing an exhaustive work of academic research, which would have taken me a time which I do not have. I believe Economics is a behavioural science, so the text is full of argumentations assuming that we all behave rationally in the achievement of our objectives. In the same vein, although running the risk of not presenting sound empirical evidence, I have not used Econometrics in the text, which would otherwise become too complex to read (and to write for me!).

Besides, I have also tried to be clear in explanations and not to pre-judge any of the behaviours observed during the financial crisis. That is to say, I have just attempted to present a neutral argumentation of what has happened since 2008 and of the proposals to return to normal times, using simple premises and relying always on information publicly available. It has not been my purpose to solely blame anybody for the financial crisis.

The scope of the following pages covers financial markets in general, understood as the places where financial instruments (shares, bonds, derivatives and others) are exchanged. Given their special role in financial markets, special attention is paid to financial institutions, in general, and to banks, in particular. This explains that in the text several terms (financial institutions, banks, reporting entities,...) are used to refer to the entities under discussion in a particular section.

The whole text is written in English, which is not my mother tongue. Nevertheless, I chose to write in Shakespeare's language in order to reach a broader audience, as English has become nowadays the global language. Not being my mother tongue, I am sure I have made many mistakes in trying to express my ideas. My apologies in advance for that, I hope that at least my mistakes are not too hard for the eyes of those who share mother tongue with Shakespeare.

The book is organized as follows. A short description of the financial crisis, with a focus on the European Union, is provided in Chapter I. Chapter II discusses a phenomenon which has remained largely unnoticed for the public but which has terribly changed financial markets: the use of computers. The role of unaddressed conflicts of interest is described in Chapter III. As most of the content of this text is focused on banks, Chapter IV makes the case for the existence of capital requirements for banks, which differentiates them from other sectors of activity like car manufacturing. So far, these are mainly descriptive chapters. From this point onwards, the book moves towards more policy-oriented areas. Chapter V discusses some of the policy options which are now on the table of regulators and supervisors worldwide. Finally, Chapter VI develops the decisive role which incentives and the values in our society play in the functioning of financial markets.

Last but not least, this is the modest product of my work during several months. I have extensively discussed it with Andrea and she has provided very valuable comments. All remaining errors in the text are, needless to say, my own. And in a text of more than 29.000 words, statistically speaking, there shall be many of them.

Fragile like Glass

Chapter 1: On the Brink of Financial Meltdown

And Darkness and Decay and the Red Death held illimitable dominion over all.

The Masque of Read Death (1842), Edgar Allan Poe

Much has been written about the financial crisis which widely erupted in 2008 and which has hit since then, with short illusory periods of "return-to-normal", the entire world. As in many previous crises before, it is not possible to identify a unique cause of the crisis, but a combination of several factors, some of which stem back as far as the 1980s, which took the financial system and the economy to the situation where it currently stands. The nature and effects of the crisis have been different in the US, where it originated, and in Europe, where acute imbalances in the banking and in the public sectors have been brought to light. In addition to them, several conflicts of interest, which were not adequately addressed in due time, and recent trends in capital regulation have contributed to the financial turmoil we have witnessed in the last five years.

Before entering into further details, the following pages aim at providing an overall picture of how the financial sector was brought to a situation of quasi-meltdown, with a focus on the origin of the crisis in the US mortgage-based securities and on some changes to the legal framework under which banks operated in the US. This chapter finishes with a description of the crisis in the European Union.

Fragile like Glass

1. The perfect storm

A combination of many factors, some of which are discussed in the following pages, some others which are not discussed here and even some others still unknown, brought the financial system, and the world, very close to collapse in the last days of summer and the early autumn of 2008. The crisis got its higher point in September 2008 with the collapse of Lehman Brothers, which brought several days of chaos to the financial system worldwide. It is very difficult to summarize all the different episodes of the crisis since then, but the following paragraphs try to provide an overall picture of this chain of events.

These events were triggered by the difficulties, in 2007, of some investment funds of Bear Stearns, in the US, which operated with newly-designed mortgage-based securities[1], following concerns about the real quality of the underlying securities. Afterwards, the market of mortgage-based securities started to be much volatile and fire sales[2] escalated. Widespread fire sales brought down the prices of the securities and their holders started to incur into significant losses as a consequence of the decrease in price. In some cases, these losses started to add to significant amounts in comparison with capital held and the profits from other

---

[1] Broadly speaking, the mechanism consisted of packing a whole set of mortgages, where only few of them were of the highest quality, but enough to grant the highest rating to the package. The packed mortgages were sold to investors, with different returns depending on whether the investors were paid in the first place as mortgages were paid back or later in the hierarchy. Needless to say, those getting the money from the last mortgages in the package were promised a higher return, although the risk of never being paid was certainly high.

[2] The term "fire sales" refers to the sale of goods at very low prices, usually due to the financial difficulties of the seller, which is in a hurry to get money from these goods.

activities of the banks. Some banks started to post losses in their accounting financial statements, a fact which was not well-received by investors and markets, and which deteriorated further their situation. In addition to that, based on these concerns, the provision of liquidity halted for some institutions as well.

When defaults started to spread through the markets, the holders of Credit-Default-Swaps (CDS)[3] went back to the sellers of these derivatives, in order to claim the repayment foreseen in the contracts. It was then found out that most of the CDS contracts had been sold by a subsidiary of an US insurance corporation (AIG), which soon afterwards was not able to honor its commitments. As a consequence, many holders of CDS did not benefit from the protection the CDS promised to them.

What seemed to be a crisis in a specific part of the financial markets, soon showed its real face when Lehman Brothers was left to collapse. In the days after it, panic spread throughout the world as nobody could know with certainty to which Lehman Brothers was exposed. The fall of Lehman Brothers also accelerated injections of public capital into the most troubled and least capitalized institutions, which were merged among them or sold to sound competitors. In the US, the TARP (Trouble Asset Relief Programme), which provided substantial public support to troubled banks via purchase of the most troubled assets, was drafted in hours overnight, because the main banks in the US were literally falling apart. In the US, in the UK and to a lesser extent in other countries of the EU, the largest banking groups (and also AIG) became public in a matter of days, and, in some of them, the government still holds a majority of the shares.

---

[3] Credit Default Swaps (CDS) are contracts where the seller of the contract commits himself to compensate the buyer of the contract in the event that a third party defaults.

Fragile like Glass

In Europe, in general, these movements were seen as concerning only some investment banks in the US. However, the crisis soon reached Europe, mainly via the widespread loss of confidence amidst participants in the financial markets, a logical reaction which followed the collapse of Lehman Brothers. In those days, the real situation of banks was not known and fear was everywhere, so banks decided not to borrow to each other or, if so, to ask for higher protection measures. There was not a clear view of the real situation of banks and even supervisors found some surprises among the banks under their scrutiny. As a consequence of these fears, the short-term interbank market froze and the fragile situation of many European sovereigns and banks was brought into the light. The response by political EU authorities to these unfavourable events was slow, passive, uncoordinated and domestically-oriented. Consequently, the markets were not reassured at all and a negative feedback loop arose. The result of this has been a long recession in Europe, where unemployment is reaching record levels.

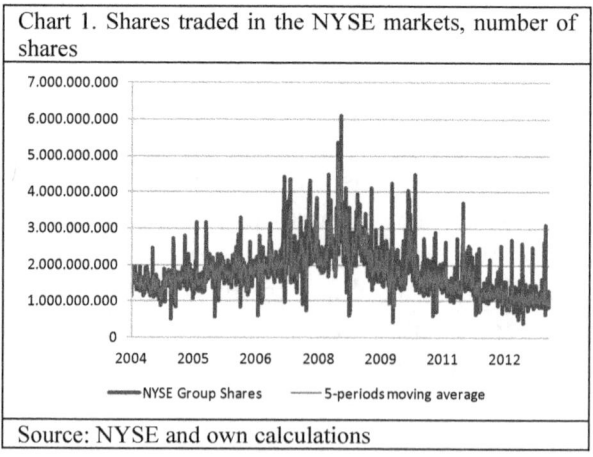

More than five years after the collapse of Lehman Brothers, the situation has not improved much. The financial market has become more concentrated, as many mergers and acquisitions have taken place since then. The financial system is now confronted with larger-in-size and fewer-in-number institutions, multiplying the risk derived from the "Too-Big-To-Fail" status, which may even become "Too-Big-To-Save". In general terms, the activity in financial markets has not decreased significantly and remains just shortly below the levels it had prior to 2008 (see, for example, Charts 1, disclosing the number of shares traded in the New York stock market, and 2, which shows the cross-border activities of banks[4]).

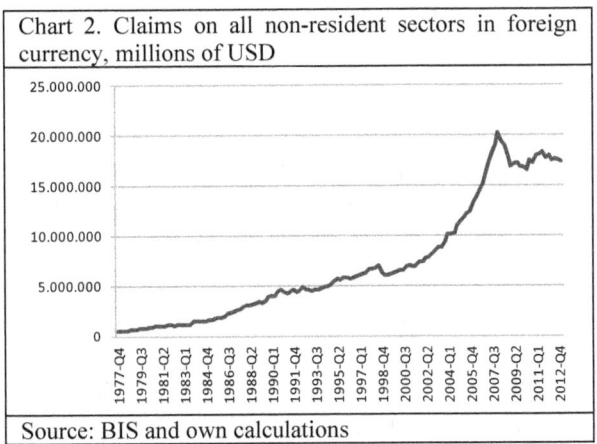

Chart 2. Claims on all non-resident sectors in foreign currency, millions of USD

Source: BIS and own calculations

Furthermore, the confidence in financial markets has not returned and most of the transactions are now entered only when collateral or any other form of protection (secured funding) is provided. Levels of activity in the interbank market remain low and transactions are only possible between known counterparts. The overall trust which governed most of the unsecured funding before the crisis is gone and not expected to return. Values well below 1 of

---

[4] The cross-border activity of banks is a good indicator of the confidence and trust among banks. The current crisis has evidenced that in periods of uncertainty, financial markets become fragmented and banks mainly return to their domestic markets.

the ratio of market capitalization to book value still show the existing uncertainty about the health of the banks[5].

Looking at the public sector, the situation is far from normal. First, some governments still hold a significant amount of shares of several large banks. Second, after the support given by governments to banks, some of them are experiencing severe budget problems, which are even bringing them close to default. These budget problems are imposing further severe cuts in other expenses within the public budget, in order to allow the public debt to return to a sustainable path.

Worldwide, the financial crisis has brought severe recessions to many economies, bringing them to production levels of ten years before. Industrial production and international trade have decreased, unemployment worldwide has soared (reaching standing rates of around 25% in Spain or Greece), and, for the first time in many years, it is possible that the next generation will endure harder living conditions than the previous one. In this scenario, it is not surprising that extreme political options are rising in the Western hemisphere. Thus, the situation is nowadays far from being "back-to-normal" or, better said, is moving towards a "new normal".

Moreover, the financial crisis evidenced that the growth in the previous years was sustained in a very fragile equilibrium, despite the self-complacency which reigned among the supervisory and

---

[5] The price to book value ratio compares the valuation of a given company in the financial markets with the value from the accounting financial statements. Ideally, both valuations should coincide or be very close to each other. A value below 1 indicates that the market is undervaluing the company, when compared to the value in accounts, due to, among others, some negative issues which are not disclosed in the accounting financial statements. A value over 1 reflects an overvaluation of the company in the financial markets, which is not reflected in the accounting figures.

regulatory community. Many imbalances were silently growing in those years and the crisis of mortgage-based securities was only a trigger, but any other event could have triggered similar effects. In policy terms, beyond some grandiloquent expressions at the height of the crisis by political leaders, the response to some of the issues which the crisis highlighted as insufficiently addressed is being rather timid and uncoordinated.

Before progressing further, we will have a closer look at some regulatory changes in the US which brought some unintended consequences many years later and at the nature and effects of the financial crisis in Europe. A closer look at the US situation would help us understand why the mortgage-based securities were the trigger for the crisis while the analysis of the effects of the crisis in the EU will help to understand why some European sovereigns have been so much distressed by the financial crisis.

2. Once upon a time in America

One of the consequences of the Great Depression, back to 1929, was the introduction of the Glass-Steagall Act, which restricted the business where banks could operate, in an attempt to protect the deposits of citizens from losses generated in the trading activities of banks. As a consequence of the Glass-Steagall Act, universal banks, understood as those taking deposits from individuals and actively trading complex financial products, were not possible in the US. Therefore, investment and commercial banks were legally forced to develop separately. Nonetheless, in the 1980s a strong movement for the repeal of the Glass-Steagall Act gained force, which finally succeeded in removing the separation between retail and investment banking activities. As explained later in this text, in those years, there was an excess of liquidity in the financial system, which was some kind of an invitation for banks to expand into new areas of business, something to which the existent Glass-Steagall Act imposed limitations.

Consequently, a number of commercial banks (Citigroup, Bank of America, among others) started soon afterwards to engage in lines of business which were at the core of investment banking. The movement of investment banks into commercial banking activities was, although existent, more limited. The repeal of the Glass-Steagall Act had significant consequences in the functioning of the US banking sector, which effects were felt worldwide.

First, new actors came to the stage, a fact which increased competence and reduced margins. In economic theory, competence is welcome and is one of the main benefits of free market, since it pushes down prices and optimizes the benefit for customers. On the contrary, in monopolies and oligopolies, companies can charge any price they wish to their customers; in free market competence drives down prices and benefits for producers. For the customers, the introduction of new actors into the areas of investment and commercial banking meant that they had a wider range of banks with which they could deal and, therefore, could make some pressure on the interests of loans and deposits and on the fees charged. Consequently, the margins of the banks, income minus expenses, diminished.

Chart 3 below shows how interest margins of large US banks (blue bars) diminished in the period 2002-2009 while the amount of total assets was growing significantly (orange line), what implies that banks had to own more assets to obtain the same profit. In other words, profit of US banks came from an increase in size (volume) and not from the margins of the transactions, which were indeed rather narrow (always below 4%).

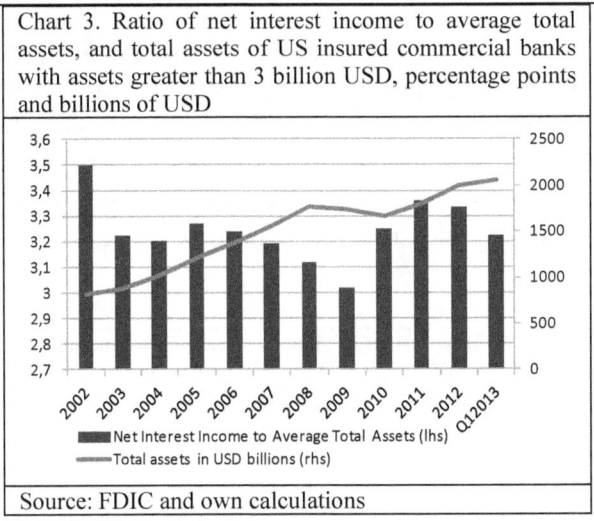

Chart 3. Ratio of net interest income to average total assets, and total assets of US insured commercial banks with assets greater than 3 billion USD, percentage points and billions of USD

Source: FDIC and own calculations

This reduction of margins may partly explain some of the mergers and acquisitions which happened soon afterwards, as banks tried to generate synergies which could reduce their administrative and operational costs to maintain a level of profits adequate for the shareholders, compensating the negative effect of the reduction in the margins. Another way of keeping the profits in satisfactory levels for the shareholders was to enter into more risky transactions, which are able to generate more income but which have higher underlying risks. That is to say, a movement of search-for-yield started, on the basis of financial innovation: creating new instruments capable of keeping costs (also in terms of regulatory capital) at a minimum, while generating more income than traditional products. The complex mortgaged-backed securities which exploded in 2008 were just the latest development in this phenomenon of search-for-yield.

Second, some commercial banks entered into the businesses of investment banking as "an elephant in a glass-shop". They lacked the expertise and the know-how to operate in these areas, but, on the other hand, they had a tremendous amount of resources

Fragile like Glass

available: deposits from customers. Chart 4 displays the evolution of the growth rates of short-term investments and short-term non-core funding (basically, non-deposits) for the largest US banks. It can be seen how the short-term investments grew at a more acute pace than the short-term non-core funding, implying that some core funding (deposits) was used to fund these growing short-term investments.

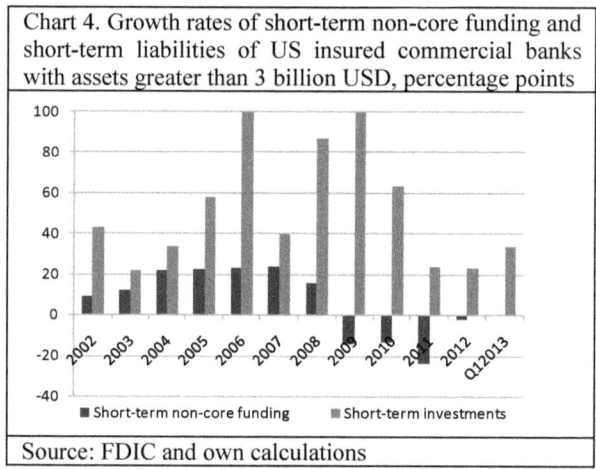

Chart 4. Growth rates of short-term non-core funding and short-term liabilities of US insured commercial banks with assets greater than 3 billion USD, percentage points

Source: FDIC and own calculations

Commercial banks were more used to traditional retail activities and they could not fully capture the risks involved in the complex operations they were starting to get engaged in. The same was true for some Chief Executive Officers (CEOs) of traditional investment banks (Lewis, 2012). In some cases, commercial banks were misguided by the employees they hired, whose personal interests were not always fully aligned with those of the bank. In some other cases, they just played the role of the "necessary fool" in many operations, where commercial banks took just the portion of the cake which nobody else wanted to have[6].

---

[6] From conversations with employees of investment banks in those years, Lewis (2012) uses the term "Düsseldorf fools" to refer to German banks which bought the worst

So far, in the US banking system, the repeal of the Glass-Steagall Act led to an intense competence which negatively affected profits and the subsequent reaction in terms of search-for-yield. Additionally, some participants in investment banking lacked the required know-how of the business. The picture looks like pretty dangerous already, but there is still more to come.

During the 80s a new remuneration policy emerged and soon became quite popular among bankers. This new approach to remuneration combined a fixed amount with a variable amount to be paid depending on the evolution of a benchmark. In most cases, the accounting profit of the year was set as this benchmark. Therefore, the final payroll of bankers started to depend on the accounting profit generated by the bank thanks to their management. The original intention of this policy was well-intended (to reward bank managers who work hard and generate profit for the shareholders), but soon it showed that it was prone to misuse.

As profits were the only drivers of the variable remuneration of bankers, they (probably unconsciously) changed their approach to the management of the bank. Profits became more prominent and other parameters, such as risks incurred or long-term consequences of the decisions, started to be less and less considered. Therefore, banks started to enter into more risky transactions which generated more profits in the short-term, but which in the long-term may not be so attractive (namely, the orange bars in Chart 4), and bankers were generously rewarded for that. In any case, managers would leave the bank in five or ten years and they would not witness the long-term effects of some of their riskier decisions. With time, the

---

tranche of mortgage-based securities. The phenomenon was not limited to German banks, but serves to provide an idea of how sophisticated investment bankers treated some of their partners in these transactions.

Fragile like Glass

variable component of the payroll grew in size and was more important than the fixed amount. Its success in the first years also meant that it spread within banks, not being limited any more to high management but reaching areas such as trading desks.

Then, to sum up, as outlined by Schema 1, these initiatives generated a search-for-yield behaviour, a limited knowledge by a significant part of the market of the more complex financial products and remuneration policies which focused solely on short-term profits. Another consequence was a process of mergers and acquisitions, which reduced the number of institutions in the market and marked the birth of the "Too-Big-To-Fail" category, well before this label would become famous worldwide.

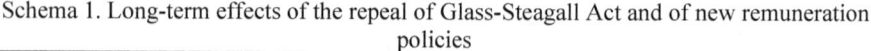
Schema 1. Long-term effects of the repeal of Glass-Steagall Act and of new remuneration policies
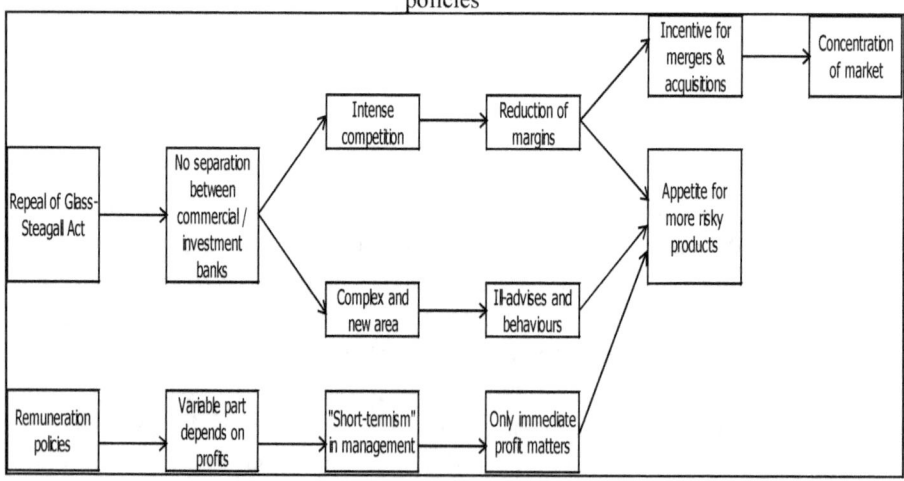

3. Collateral damage in the EU

The financial crisis has dramatically hit Europe, expanding its scope to reach some sovereign countries and putting into question even the Economic and Monetary Union (EMU) itself. The largest European banks certainly followed the behaviour of their US counterparts, as described in previous pages, and the effects of the crisis have been similar for them. However, there are a number of features in Europe which explain why financial crisis has so severely hit sovereign countries. The following paragraphs try to discuss how and why the European sovereign crisis erupted.

Box 1. Reserve currencies

Currencies (such as dollars, euros, pounds, dinars or rubles) are basically promises of the Central Bank of the country of the currency to pay, upon demand, the holder of the note or coin the amount expressed in it. The acceptance of currencies worldwide depends hence mostly on the credibility of its Central Bank and its ability to honour this promise.

In this vein, some currencies are more widely used than others, because they are quoted in financial markets with no restriction and they are free of devaluations (decreases of the value of the currency, carried out by the government, in order to benefit exports of the country), re-denominations (division of the value of the currency by 1.000 following many years of high inflation) or similar actions which can diminish at any time, without prior notice, its value. For example, for these reasons, the worldwide acceptance of the US dollars (USD[7]) is higher than that of the Burmese kyat (MMK).

---

[7] There is a myriad of acronyms to refer to currencies. Here we use the usual convention of three characters, the first two for the country and the third one for the name

Fragile like Glass

> In those cases where a currency is highly regarded by financial markets (receiving the name of "reserve currency"), the country issuing it does not have problems finding somebody to use it, so the country does not need to worry too much about its macroeconomic variables: it can just print more banknotes and somebody will buy them in order to have an stock of the reserve currency. For example, the deficit of US and Japan is growing year after year and the respective countries seem to do little to contain it. This is because there is always somebody willing to buy dollars or yens, be it the public of a Latin America indebted country, Chinese investors, the Japanese households or Arab countries exporters of oil. From a certain point of view, the reputation built around these reserve currencies weights more than the fundamentals of the country of the reserve currency.

A. A fake illusion: the euro as reserve currency

Prior to the introduction of the euro (EUR), the US dollar (USD), the Japanese yen (JPY), the British pound (GBP), the Swiss franc (CHF) and the German mark (DEM) were widely considered as reserve currencies. Once the euro came into force, it was then assumed to inherit the status of reserve currency from the German mark. Therefore, those countries participating in the euro which did not have a reserve currency before (actually, all except Germany) did benefit greatly from the introduction of the euro, as they started to enjoy the benefits of having a reserve currency, a status which their national currencies could never dream to have. Therefore, pressure over their deficit and debt diminished significantly and they benefited from large entries of flows of international investment. To put it simple, it was as if Germany had extended its reputation to all the euro zone countries.

---
of the currency.

Before proceeding further, it is worth noting that the notion of reserve currencies can also serve to explain the little interest of the United Kingdom in joining the euro zone. Its authorities have clearly seen that the day they join, the GBP will lose its status as reserve currency and the United Kingdom will lose its privileged situation. In other words, United Kingdom has little to win from the introduction of the euro. These dynamics explain as well why Spain and United Kingdom are so differently considered by the financial markets even if their fundamentals are rather similar.

Going back to the issue of the euro as a reserve currency, Chart 5 displays the spread between the 10-year government bond of Spain, Italy and Greece with the German 10-year government bond, which is taken as benchmark (the risk premia)[8].

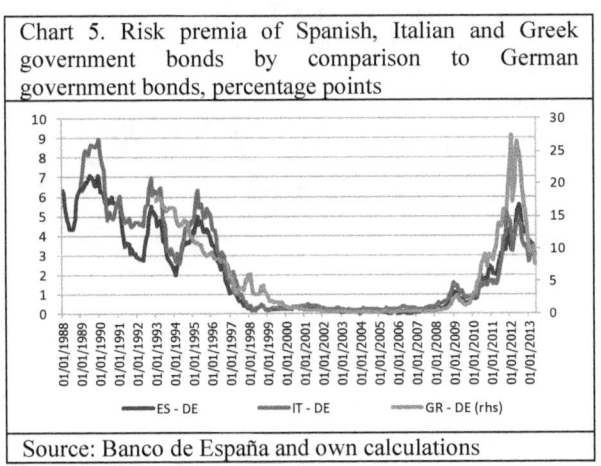

Chart 5. Risk premia of Spanish, Italian and Greek government bonds by comparison to German government bonds, percentage points

Source: Banco de España and own calculations

It can be observed how the spread was rather high when the three Mediterranean countries (which already were members of the

---

[8] This difference is usually called the "risk premia" because it depicts the additional price to pay for an asset in comparison of a risk-free asset, which, in this case, is assumed to be the 10-year German government bond.

Fragile like Glass

EU) had their local currencies and how, once the expectations of the introduction of the euro started to grow, the spread diminished to a level close to zero for the three countries in 1999. The spread remained in that level almost ten years, until the turmoil in financial markets started to put into question the sustainability of the public finances of some euro zone countries. It can be seen how during ten years Spain, Italy and Greece were getting long-term financing at similar rates than Germany. It seems as if the status of reserve currency of the DEM was understood to be extended to the EUR. However, the financial crisis and the uncoordinated and weak political response by the EU highlighted the limitations of the monetary union and the overall status of the EUR as reserve currency disappeared, being restricted again to Germany.

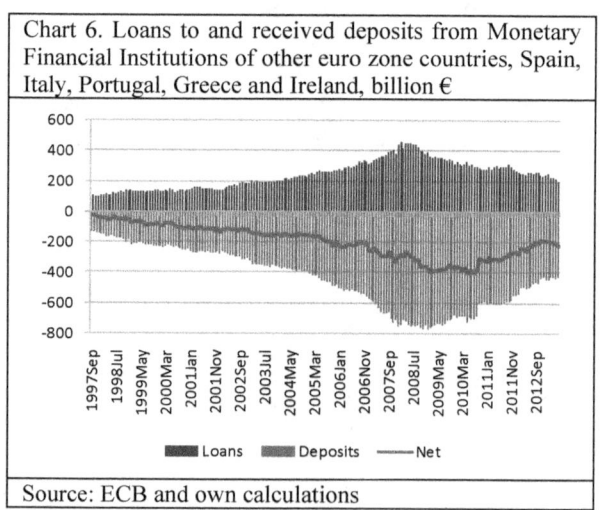

Chart 6. Loans to and received deposits from Monetary Financial Institutions of other euro zone countries, Spain, Italy, Portugal, Greece and Ireland, billion €

Source: ECB and own calculations

The more favourable conditions for the financing of the debt were not limited to the governments of Spain, Italy and Greece. Indeed, also non-financial corporations, financial institutions and households in these countries saw how the cost of borrowing decreased significantly following the establishment of the euro as currency, what implied the removal of controls on financial flows and the inability to carry out de- and revaluations. In these countries, a new world of possibilities, to be financed with debt, opened up. Chart 6 above shows the evolution of the loans and deposits to and from banks in other countries of the euro zone for the banking systems of Spain, Italy, Greece, Portugal and Ireland. It can be observed how the negative net amount (loans minus deposits) reached a peak in 2008-2009, after a standing increase in previous years. In other words, these five countries were the destination of substantial funds from banks in the same euro zone, which had too much liquidity and decided to invest important amounts of money into them[9].

Once we have seen that indeed a huge transfer of funds came to some euro zone countries in the years following the introduction of the euro, the immediate question refers to what these countries did with the new funds. Here these five countries can be grouped in two groups: one of them containing Spain and Ireland, and the other Portugal, Greece and Italy.

As shown in Chart 7 below, the total Spanish economy started to move to significant negative balances between financial assets and liabilities[10] from 2001, reaching the maximum value in 2008. Most of this change was driven by non-financial corporations (which include those operating in the sector of real estate), as they had now easier access to funds, either via financial markets directly or via banks (financial institutions). From 2008 onwards, a

---

[9] It is also interesting to look at the values in the last observations. It can be observed how the net between loans and deposits has decreased significantly, to levels not seen since 2005. This fact could point to the recent fragmentation of the euro zone financial markets as a consequence of the financial crisis, already signaled by many.

[10] Net financial assets and liabilities of a given sector cover all financial assets which are owned by entities belonging to that sector as well as all financial liabilities (debt) incurred. These two variables do not necessarily match, as the difference may be covered by other variables, such as non-financial assets or government transfers.

Fragile like Glass

moderate process of reduction in the indebtedness of the total economy can be appreciated (although with a significant deterioration for the sector of Public Administration). The case of Ireland is similar to that of Spain.

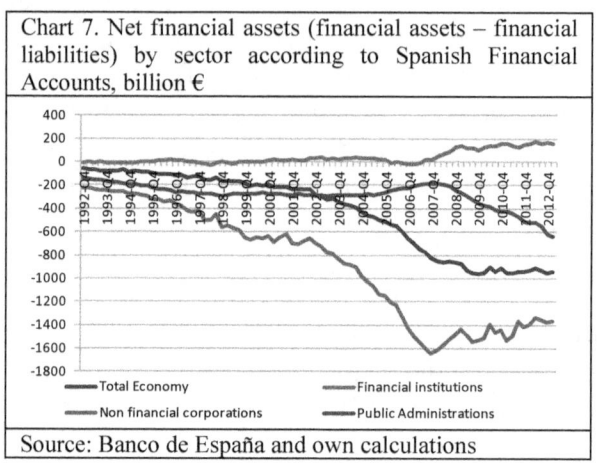

Chart 7. Net financial assets (financial assets – financial liabilities) by sector according to Spanish Financial Accounts, billion €

Source: Banco de España and own calculations

On the contrary, Italy, Portugal and Greece did not experience an economic boom from these inflows to their economies, but rather continued to show modest growth rates in the GDP and significant public deficits (see Chart 8). Inflows did not push these economies upwards (average growth rates of the GDP are negative for the three countries) and mainly served, in this case, to alleviate the burden on excessive debt on their economies, financing thus long-standing imbalances.

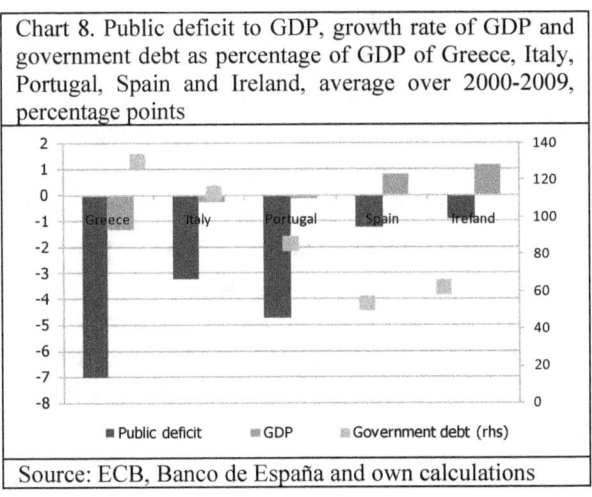

Chart 8. Public deficit to GDP, growth rate of GDP and government debt as percentage of GDP of Greece, Italy, Portugal, Spain and Ireland, average over 2000-2009, percentage points

Source: ECB, Banco de España and own calculations

To sum up, financial markets assumed that the EUR inherited the condition of reserve currency from the DEM (also due to the convergence criteria which were aimed at bringing other euro zone countries closer to Germany), what drove down the cost of debt in all euro zone countries not being Germany. Consequently, the economies of these countries got heavily indebted, profiting from the new conditions which equaled them to Germany. In other words, country risk virtually disappeared within the euro zone. When the financial crisis erupted, the weak and uncoordinated response by the EU did not persuade financial markets that the EUR was a real reserve currency, leaving these Mediterranean countries in trouble: highly indebted, with large imbalances and with worsening conditions for the funding of their debt.

B. Financing the Mediterranean gaiety

In previous paragraphs, we have gone through the increase of debt in some Mediterranean countries following the extension of the status of foreign currency from the DEM to the EUR. But who provided the money to, for example, Spanish non-financial

Fragile like Glass

corporations to increase their indebtedness? Well, the fact that Mediterranean countries were perceived by the market as risky as Germany attracted important flows of money into them. In most cases, investments in Spain, Italy or Greece were more profitable than investments in Germany and other similar countries, while the risk of these investments was priced at similar levels in the markets. The financial markets had the wrong perception that they were all bearing the same risk and that in case of trouble other countries in the euro zone would step in. Moreover, as outlined in the previous section for the US, these investments were driven by short-termism, that is, the search of quick profits in the short-term; they were not much committed in the long-term. As the financial crisis showed, when uncertainty and risks made these investments unattractive, these investors simply flew away.

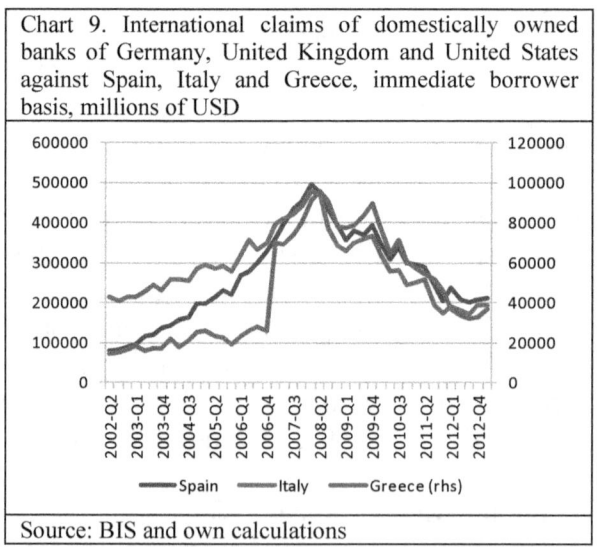

Chart 9. International claims of domestically owned banks of Germany, United Kingdom and United States against Spain, Italy and Greece, immediate borrower basis, millions of USD

Source: BIS and own calculations

Chart 9 above shows the positions of German, British and American banks (countries considered as having a reserve currency) towards Spanish, Italian and Greek banks, as reported by the Bank of International Settlements. A significant increase in the flow of funds into these three countries can be observed in the period 2002-2007[11], implying that German, British and American banks were funding the domestic sectors of these three Mediterranean countries needed for their new operations. As soon as problems in the EU erupted in 2010 and concerns about some countries were spread, the funds entering these three Mediterranean countries went back to more modest levels, in the line of those of ten years ago.

Within the euro zone, Chart 10, which is the same as Chart 6 but with a different set of countries, evidences that some countries in the euro zone (Germany, Luxembourg, the Netherlands, Austria and Finland) have maintained persistent positive balances with other countries in the euro zone. That is to say, seen together with Chart 6, the introduction of the euro gave rise to an intensification of intra euro zone flows amidst banks of different countries, with a clear transfer between Northern countries and Mediterranean countries. It seems that the excessive indebtedness in Mediterranean countries of those years was partially covered with funds from other euro zone countries. What must be clear by now is that the building-up of imbalances in the years before the crisis was not only an internal issue of each one of those countries, but was determined by foreign (often within the euro area) flows of capital.

---

[11] In the case of exposures to Greece, data from Germany is available only from 2007, what explains the significant increase observed in that period.

Fragile like Glass

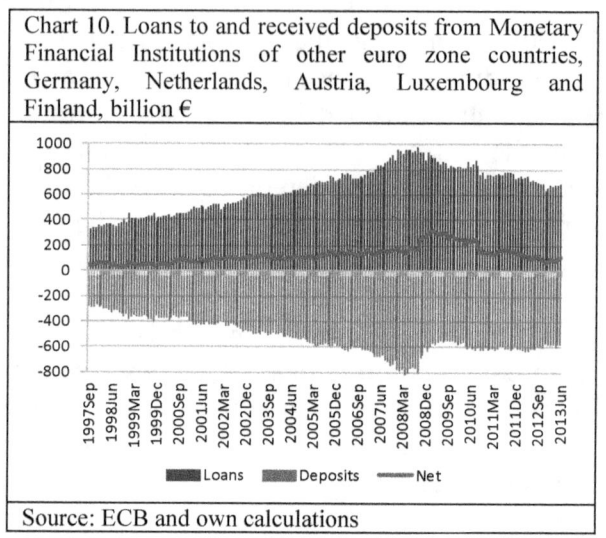

Chart 10. Loans to and received deposits from Monetary Financial Institutions of other euro zone countries, Germany, Netherlands, Austria, Luxembourg and Finland, billion €

Source: ECB and own calculations

Such an important flow of funds towards Mediterranean countries was derived from the removal of obstacles to the free flow of capital and to a number of chances for high profits which other euro zone countries could not offer. This unveiled certain euphoria around the Mediterranean countries and created a false sense of "safety" around them. When the financial crisis erupted, this euphoria disappeared and the Mediterranean countries were left highly indebted and with a significant reduction in the funds they got from abroad and to which their economies had become addicted. How the story continues is well-known by all of us, so we stop here.

Chapter 2: Financial Markets for All

Never send a human to do a machine's job.

Agent Smith, The Matrix

The introduction of information technologies (that is to say, computers) has led to an outstanding and, at the same time, silent development of financial markets, which has had severe consequences on its functioning and on how they interact among themselves and with the real economy. As a consequence of this process, financial transactions have significantly increased in number in the last years, creating a kind of separate world, where the link with the real economy is weaker and weaker. The way these new financial markets respond to crisis is also different from previous crisis and from what is expected from economic theory.

The following paragraphs aim at describing this process and how it has changed the conduct in financial markets, concluding with a short reflection on the effects of these changes.

4. Rise of the machines

Computers have dramatically changed the way financial markets work. It would not be correct to say that the financial crisis was caused by them, but the effect that the use of computers have had in the last 30 years in the financial markets cannot be ignored when discussing the current financial crisis. In this period of time, a

Fragile like Glass

substantial, but mostly hidden for the public, change has taken place, in terms which are difficult to imagine.

Up to the last years of the 1980s, trading in financial markets took place with the necessary intermediation of brokers and dealers, which acted on behalf of customers for a fee, or on their own name. Brokers and dealers met in stock markets and agreed on the transactions, basically, on a face-to-face basis. The typical image of the stock market with dozens of men shouting buy and sell orders in a frenetic dynamic was how the financial markets worked in reality. The possibility that a household could buy securities abroad or even in a different market was full of difficulties and obstacles. Intraday trading was only possible for the most sophisticated investors. Therefore, a reduced number of brokers and dealers, physically connected to only one market, acted as a bottleneck, since all transactions have to go necessarily through them. In those years, information about prices was scarce and paperwork was a heavy duty before and after entering a transaction. Basically, the only trading strategy which was possibly was to invest on a long-term horizon, mostly based on the characteristics of the company (in line with classical economic theory).

Computers started to be introduced in the 1990s as a quicker way to provide brokers and dealers with information about prices of securities, in a format which could be easily processed by computers. Soon afterwards, the amount of information transmitted allowed some of them to design trading strategies which tried to benefit from loopholes and small spreads in the prices. Step by step, in a process which took years to complete, access to this information was widened, opening new business opportunities for brokers and dealers. So, trading platforms, which allow any kind of investor to trade in many different markets, were created. This process increased the competence among brokers and dealers, which now were fighting for the design of the best trading strategies and platforms. Consequently, buyers and sellers did no longer have to physically meet in the same place, but could work remotely from any corner in the world. In other words, in 2005, it was possible to trade any security listed in any market in the world from a computer at home[12].

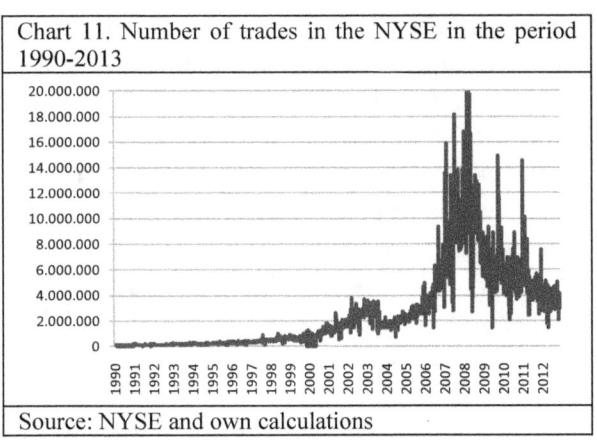

Chart 11. Number of trades in the NYSE in the period 1990-2013

Source: NYSE and own calculations

Data from the New York Stock Exchange (NYSE) serves to evidence how this process changed the shape of the operations in stock markets. From 1990 onwards, the number of trades per day increased substantially (see Chart 11[13]). On 11 May 1990, the number of trades was higher than 100,000 for the first time; on 16 September 1997 the number was higher than 500,000 for the first time; and on 1 January 2007 it was over 5,000,000 trades for the first time, reaching a peak of 20,000,000 trades in 2008. Since most stock markets earned a fee per trade, it is easy to guess how their income increased as well with this increase in trading, a fact which had a direct impact in their willingness to keep this trend moving

---

[12] See Patterson (2012) for a more detailed description of this process.
[13] Due to a break in the time series, data from 2004 onwards are not fully comparable with data from previous years.

and in their lack of interest in having a closer look at the potential risks and vulnerabilities arising from these new practices.

In the financial markets which we have right now, algorithm trading and high-frequency-trading (HFT) are just two terms to describe the trading driven by computers, which uses massive amounts of data to find opportunities in the market which a human being is not able to capture. Orders of considerable size are posted in milliseconds and, in most cases, are withdrawn at the same speed. The starting point of these strategies is a small spread between buy and sell prices, often amounting only to a cent of a dollar. Such a spread is not significant individually considered, but when the order covers millions or even billions of shares, the profit generated is remarkable. When the same operation is repeated thousands of time per day, the profit at the end of the day may be quite significant.

Consequently, the stock markets have started to look like game hunting, where HFT and algorithm traders are trying to discover big whales, large and slow orders placed by institutional investors (for example, pension funds), in order to benefit from a spread seconds before these large orders are executed. One of the logical reactions of these large institutional investors has been to split their orders into pieces, trying to make them invisible to other market participants. The consequence of that has been, as shown by Chart 12, that the average amount of dollars per each trade has been falling significantly since year 2000, which approximately marks the start of HFT and algorithm trading strategies. It is clear that this behaviour of institutional investors is not the only reason for the reduction of size in orders but it is a decisive contributing factor.

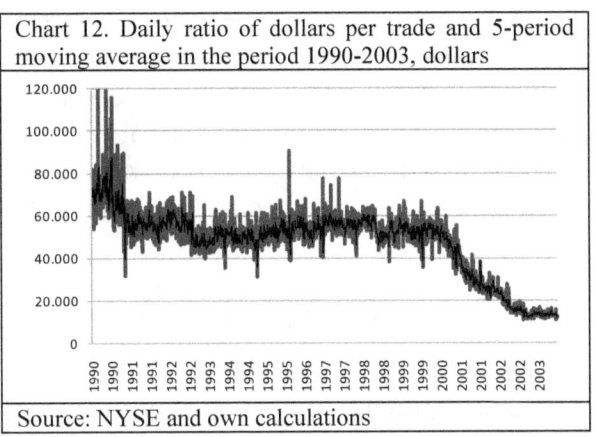

Chart 12. Daily ratio of dollars per trade and 5-period moving average in the period 1990-2003, dollars

Source: NYSE and own calculations

Finally, it is worth referring briefly to the development of over-the-counter (OTC) markets and dark pools for securities. The main characteristic of both OTC markets and dark pools is the fact that they are not regulated markets. Indeed, they are based on bilateral relations among counterparties; where there is no need to publicly disclose any detail of the transaction. From a certain point of view, these markets are at the margins of the regulated markets. As mentioned earlier, HFT and algorithm traders started to hunt big orders from institutional investors in order to get a spread from it. This hunt made that institutional investors started to look at places outside the regulated markets, mainly at dark pools, in areas out of the reach of the HFT and algorithm traders. Therefore, in the years prior to the crisis, they were more recurrently used by these institutional investors and when the crisis erupted, supervisors and regulators found themselves not knowing what exactly was going on there. The fact of negotiating bilaterally outside the financial markets is not harmful *per se*; the threat comes from the fact that excessive trading in OTC markets or in dark pools make regulated financial markets not representative of the real demand and supply of financial assets, damaging the mechanism of formation of prices, and, at the same time, hamper the ability of regulators and supervisors of following developments in the financial system. Current efforts to introduce some common basic regulation and disclosure in the OTC derivatives markets are certainly on the right direction, but the issue of regulating dark pools is more difficult to tackle. After all, two willing parties will always have the right to make a bilateral deal, without the need to go to a regulated market.

5. The need for speed

The quick development of High-Frequency Trading (HFT[14]) has driven stock markets to a situation where (i) large amounts of orders are placed and immediately cancelled in a matter of milliseconds, (ii) machine-driven algorithms account for a significant part of the daily trading volume, (iii) significant amounts of money are paid to markets in order to place HFT servers as closest as possible to the servers of the markets, and (iv) the market may implode before regulators can literally blink[15]. Confronted with this situation, it is worth reviewing which benefits HFT brings to the market and what can be done to reduce the negative consequences of their activities.

One of the main benefits brought by HFT is that it apparently brings liquidity to the markets, since they are literally flooded with millions of buy and sale orders. At this point, one can ask himself whether liquidity is the ultimate objective of financial markets. In the process which led to the massive participation of computers in

---

[14] HFT is used as acronym for both High-Frequency Trading, meaning the strategies of trading, and High-Frequency Traders, meaning the traders which apply High-Frequency Trading strategies. Although this section is based on High-Frequency Trading, its discussion can easily be extended to algorithm trading as well.

[15] See Haldane (2011) for an outstanding first approach to HFT.

the financial markets in the 1990s, which is described above, liquidity became the central variable of stock markets. The provision of liquidity seems to have become the main goal of financial markets, leaving aside some other principles such as the formation of fair prices or the level playing field for all kind of investors. Stock exchanges earned a profit per trade entered, so they had strong incentives to attract investors willing to actively post as many orders as possible in their markets. For some market participants, it seems that the best financial market is the most liquid one, an assessment which may not necessarily hold true in all cases.

Having said that, though, a closer look at the way HFT works shows that most of this liquidity never materialises, as the majority of the orders posted by HFT are cancelled immediately afterwards, as their only objective is to provoke a change in the price of a security. In other words, the liquidity which HFT produces in financial markets is fake, not real. Out of the millions of orders posted by HFT, only a very small proportion of them are finally entered into real transactions. HFT produces a false sense of liquidity in financial markets.

Related with the previous is the claim that HFT reduces the buy and sell spreads of securities, contributing to a better formation of prices. This argument, presented like this, is difficult to rebate but it hides how HFT behaves in reality concerning the spreads. What HFT tries to do is to gain a small benefit from artificially moving the buy and sell prices of securities, in order to benefit from spreads measured in terms of cents of euro or dollar. They try to catch small temporary spreads in the buy and sell prices of stocks, which may appear just due to small flaws in the markets. For example, imagine that, for some seconds, due to unmatched orders, the sell price of a security is 10.15 and its buy price is 10.10. The underlying rationale behind HFT is to take advantage of

Fragile like Glass

this temporary mismatch by posting a quick offer to buy at 10.10 and sell at 10.15, getting a profit of 0.05 per security in the transaction. In real life, many HFT fight for this spread and, when the spread is not there, they try to create it by misleading investors with artificial buy and sell offers, which only objective is to move other market participants (mostly those using also algorithms for trading as well) in the desired direction, creating thus the spread upon which to get the profit.

In any case, ultimately, the benefit obtained from the reduction of the spreads by HFT does not benefit retail or institutional investors and, even less, our society. More to the contrary, the benefit of HFT means a loss for investors, since they have to pay a slightly higher or lower price to buy or sell their securities, as a consequence of their "slower" connection to financial markets. HFT uses loopholes in the financial markets for their own benefit, not for the benefit of society: in the end, the spread between the sell and buy price (which represents somehow the inefficiency of the financial markets) does not disappear, but goes to the HFT. Beyond that, from a certain point of view, it can be stated that HFT introduces distortions in the financial markets, maybe not in the formation in prices (after all, the spreads upon which they base their activity are measured in cents of a dollar), but actually in volume, giving a false sense of depth to the financial markets. Indeed, the current role of HFT and the cost they impose on investors can be paralleled to the role that brokers and dealers played in the financial markets up to the 1990s, acting as bottlenecks.

Box 2. The "flash crash"

A vivid and recent example of the potential damage that widespread HFT and algorithm trading can generate is provided by the "flash crash" of 6 May 2010, where the Dow Jones Industrial Average lost suddenly 9% just to recover the previous levels minutes later. Since then, there have been similar events, although located in specific and smaller markets, such as in India. For illustrative purposes, given the extensive literature that it has generated, only the "flash crash" is discussed here.

The official report prepared by staff of the SEC and the CFTC found out that HFT exacerbated the effects of a large-scale sale of contracts. Following a first sell order on future contracts which drove their price down, many computer-driven trading strategies automatically started to cancel their positions, since the decline of these futures went beyond their backstop levels. The withdrawal of HFT from the market left virtually no liquidity in many of the main stocks and transactions had to be entered on any available price in the market. This fact led to trades being entered at amounts of 0.01 USD or 99,999 USD, because these are usual "dummy" offers posted by market participants when they are not interested in actually buying the stock but they still want to be kept in the loop. However, in this case, with the panic spreading across HFT, these "dummy" offers were the only ones in the market.

In the "flash crash", stocks in the Dow Jones index collapsed in fifteen minutes around 2pm and were able to get back to the levels previous to the "flash crash" in 15 minutes. There was no external event which could give any hint that such a decline was coming and it was not triggered by any fundamental fact. The "flash crash" occurred suddenly and the unraveling of events was so quick that nobody was able to grasp what was happening in financial markets, let alone to react to it. Fortunately, this time, the situation could be reversed within few minutes but it does not have to be always like this.

Fragile like Glass

> The "flash crash" marked a turning point in the attitude of regulators and supervisors towards the increase in volume in financial markets. The topic was brought up to their agendas and now many policies are proposed throughout the world to prevent any new "flash crash" from happening. The most terrifying aspect of it is that it happened without the intervention of human beings, but following automatic reactions by computers to market movements, and as it sank the stock market in a matter of minutes it also took it up again.

Many measures have been proposed to limit the undesired consequences of HFT. Among them, circuit-breakers (stop trading a security if its value changes more than a given amount) and implementing real-time surveillance of the markets are the most popular. Nonetheless, their effects are far from enough to protect the financial markets and their investors. Alternative options which may have a larger effect aim at establishing a limit on the number of orders which are cancelled immediately (for example, if stock markets start requiring fees for orders placed, not for trades), at limiting the speed of the transactions, at creating some latency in the settlement of deals or at adding further measures of governance, transparency and capital to firms active in HFT. Unfortunately, none of these are the kind of magic solutions which can simply solve the problem. While some of them can limit the activities of HFT in a given market, innovation in this area will go on and new niches will be found, where HFT can generate profits for the most advanced participants in the financial markets. After all, this game will not finish until regulators and supervisors give an answer to the fundamental question of whether HFT benefits the society or just the most advanced HFT investors.

To sum up, although it is clear that HFT did not cause the crisis of 2008, it has changed the financial markets in a way that makes the effects of crisis more acute, significant, widespread and immediate. The ability of supervisors and regulators to control these practices, under a real turmoil in the markets, remains to be seen.

6. Money on a merry-go-round

The development in financial markets described in the previous two sections has dramatically changed financial markets and their role in the wider picture of our society, creating, at the same time, new threats and vulnerabilities which regulators and supervisors must be able to address. The following paragraphs try, taking as basis what has been presented so far in this section, to shed light on whether and how this increased activity in financial markets has reached the real economy.

Before proceeding further, we shall remind the fact that most of the underlying traded securities are indeed issued by real corporations, in the search of funding for their entrepreneurial activities. This basic feature seems to be now a secondary factor in the scenario of fight between trading strategies presented above. In this sense, it is not difficult to get the feeling that the financial system has become a huge closed system, separated from the real economy, where flows move within it and where the ties with the real economy, which it should finance according to the classic purpose of financial markets, are much weakened.

Let's see first whether this perception is true or not. Here the lack of appropriate data makes us look at indirect indicators. Chart 13 below displays the evolution of cross-border claims of banks to other banks and to non-banks to non-residents in foreign currencies[16]

---

[16] In both Charts 13 and 14, claims in foreign currencies are used as a proxy of the international activities of banks, which are assumed to be more linked to the development

Fragile like Glass

. The first thing that catches our attention is the significant increase from the amounts first reported in 1990. Indeed, claims to banks have grown six-fold and claims to non-banks eight-fold in twenty years. While inflation can explain some of this increase, it certainly cannot hide the fact that cross-border flows of money have intensified in the last years, reaching its peak between 2007 and 2008, just when the financial crisis was about to explode. Afterwards, there has been a small reduction on international claims, but levels remain still high.

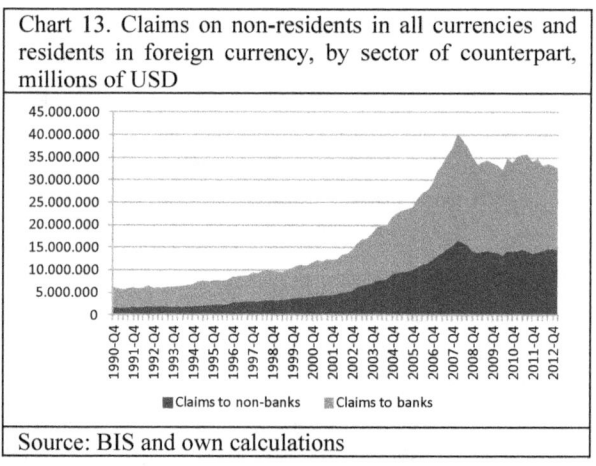

Chart 13. Claims on non-residents in all currencies and residents in foreign currency, by sector of counterpart, millions of USD

Source: BIS and own calculations

It is clear, by its own name, that claims to banks imply that nothing reaches the real economy. Regarding the definition of the non-bank sector, it mainly comprises non-financial corporations and governments as well as other financial institutions, which are often labeled as "shadow banking". From the three main sectors included in the category "non-banks", it seems that transactions with governments and, to a lesser extent, non-financial corporations are not very often entered in a cross-border basis. That is to say,

---

of the financial markets described in previous sections of this chapter than the domestic activities of banks, which are more stable in most countries.

banks do not often acquire substantial amounts of government debt from abroad in foreign currencies and they mainly deal with the non-financial corporations of their home market, since they are those they know better[17]. Consequently, the eight-fold increase observed in the chart for the claims to non-banks seems to be the result of the increase of the activity of the "shadow banking". In summary, transactions with non-resident institutions have sky-rocketed since 1990 and the drivers of such an increase seem to be transactions with other banks and with the "shadow banking", both of them belonging to the financial sector, what implies that the money involved in these transactions never actually leaves the financial system.

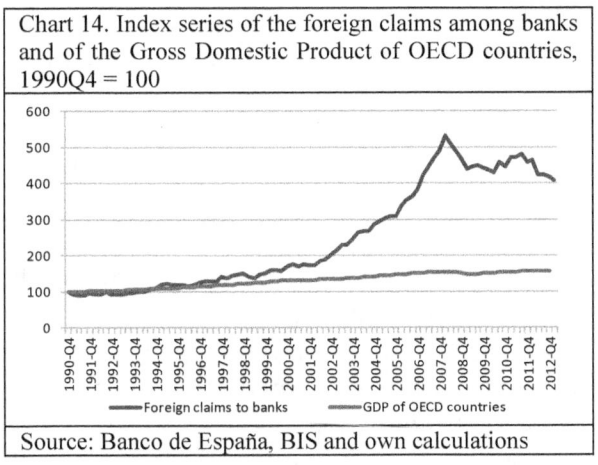

Chart 14. Index series of the foreign claims among banks and of the Gross Domestic Product of OECD countries, 1990Q4 = 100

Source: Banco de España, BIS and own calculations

The evolution of the GDP (as an indicator of the activity in the real economy) and of the flows within the financial system is compared in Chart 14. It can be observed how the flows between banks of different countries have steadily grown at a higher pace than the GDP of the countries in the OECD[18]. The fact that there

---

[17] Moreover, as shown by Chart 15 in the following pages, loans to non-financial corporations have been growing at steady and modest rates in the last twenty years.

[18] Organisation for Economic Development and Co-operation. The most advanced

has been an increase in the cross-border claims of banks since 1990 has not resulted in an equivalent increase in welfare of the society, measured using the GDP. In the period 1990-2012, foreign claims among banks have multiplied by four whereas the GDP remains below 200[19]. Even more, the GDP includes in its definition also financial institutions, which growth has not served to push the economy of OECD countries significantly upwards.

Additionally, it is worth referring briefly to the volatility of the time series of foreign claims. It is clear that the GDP cannot be, by definition volatile, but it is surprising to see how foreign claims between banks diminished approximately 20% in two years (from 2006 Q4 to 2008 Q4). Such behaviour points out that, as already commented, financial markets have become now more vulnerable and volatile.

These two charts display the growth in financial markets, which seems not to have touched much the real economy. Actually, in Western economies, the development of financial markets seems to have occurred disentangled from the growth of the economy. Consequently, it seems that the increased activity in financial markets remain within them. Following the extensive use of computers for trading, financial markets seem to have become a giant casino, a zero-gain game, where bets are placed by participants and where, for any winner, there must be a loser. Here, there are several issues around the functioning of financial markets which deserve careful thinking. The exponential increase in the number of transactions in financial markets as well as the wider range of activities and products covered generate new threats and

---

Western economies are members of the OECD. For further information, please see http://www.oecd.org.

[19] If the effect of inflation is discounted, the increase in GDP is even smaller.

vulnerabilities, which should be adequately addressed. They are briefly discussed in the next section.

7. But, tell me doctor, what does it mean to me?

So far in this section, we have presented the tremendous development of financial markets in the last 20 years, which, regardless of the crisis which erupted of 2008, has made them more vulnerable and volatile. The next question to answer is how the work of supervisors and regulators shall adjust to this new reality, in order to respond appropriately to the new challenges coming. Relying on practices which worked well in the past or resisting the necessary change may turn out to be fatal errors, which consequences will be felt hardly by the society.

First, some financial institutions are now paid for entering transactions into the market, in a search for liquidity by financial markets. As briefly touched upon in the previous section, it seems that liquidity has become the new main objective of financial markets. Financial markets are defined in Economics as the place where potential buyers and sellers meet and where they can agree a fair price for their transaction. A system where market participants are paid per transaction entered introduces perverse incentives. According to this approach, market participants may just enter transactions to gain the fee they are paid, not because they see an opportunity for investment. The classic rationale for investment is no longer used, in favour of a behaviour which tries to benefit from loopholes in the financial market, where transactions do not always reflect the fair price, with a profit which does not add any value to the society. This behaviour only leads to an increase in the number of transactions in the market. Therefore, price formation is hampered and financial markets, although liquid, depart from their basic function of aligning investors and projects to finance.

Fragile like Glass

Second, the increase in activity in financial markets derived from the extensive use of computers has increased volatility and has also reduced the time required to see the market collapse. As evidenced by the "flash crash" in 2010 (see Box 2), financial markets can now fall apart in a matter of minutes, before regulators even start to understand what is happening. The effects of the "flash crash" were quickly reversed and its overall impact was limited, but the outcome of the next crisis may not be so benevolent. At this stage, it is necessary to ask ourselves whether increasing speed and volume are really justified from a social point of view, since they seem to benefit a few but to impose costs (in terms of higher probability of sudden and severe crisis) to the society at large. In other words, the issue of whether quicker and deeper financial markets are better for the society must be answered, taking into account also the potential costs which a crisis arising from computer-driven trading activities could have.

Third, as evidenced by Chart 13, transactions between banks and entities in the "shadow banking" sector have grown significantly and are now significant enough to deserve attention from regulators and supervisors. Nonetheless, by its own name, there is not much information about the "shadow banking" sector, which comprises heterogeneous entities which usually have in common a certain degree of opaqueness in their activities. They were born far from the sight of regulators and supervisors, which considered them as marginal. However, soon these "shadow banking" entities grew and attracted more investors. At the current moment, an important proportion of all the financial transactions are taking place outside the traditional financial system and regulators and supervisors know very little about it. It is necessary thus to bring light to and to deeper analyse this sector, which has now become as significant as the regulated financial sector, since it can also be a source of threats and vulnerabilities.

Lastly, related with the previous points, financial markets are now more interconnected and speculative activities (understood as those which aim at obtaining a profit in the short-term from differences in prices, rather than having a long-term horizon) have reached markets which are not financial, such as commodities markets. Markets of oil, corn or wheat are now the common playing field of trading activities, which just hunt a quick profit and sometimes do not see the consequences of their strategies to society. For example, it is now widely accepted that an important part of the oil price is determined by the activities of future contracts on it, introducing thus a new variable in the classic model of supply and demand and, again, creating a distortion in the formation of prices. The increased interconnection of markets happens also on a geographical basis, with markets worldwide subject to the similar reactions to events happening in one corner of the world. Such interconnection, albeit desirable on the one hand, entails more vulnerable financial markets and special consideration shall be then paid to the contagion channels of crisis in one segment (geographical or by product) of the financial markets.

To conclude, it is clear that the extension to access to financial markets to the public at large has brought substantial benefits for the society and has marked the end of a situation where brokers and dealers were in a position of oligopoly. From a broader perspective, the opening of financial markets to the public has been possible thanks to the absence of capital controls in the main economies of the world. However, this extension has also generated new risks and vulnerabilities, arisen from the unintended consequences of this process, which shall be carefully monitored by supervisors and regulators. Even more, when confronted with these risks and vulnerabilities, the previous approach to the topic, where free movement of capitals was considered as the ultimate panacea, is now being questioned, with even the IMF arguing that capital

Fragile like Glass

controls may make sense in some specific cases (IMF, 2012). Certainly, the developments witnessed by financial markets in the last years have not come without new threats and dangers.

Chapter 3: Conflict of Interest

If I, taking care of everyone's interests, also take care of my own, you can't talk about a conflict of interest.

Silvio Berlusconi

A conflict of interest arises when the interest of one of the parties of any transaction clashes with the overall purpose of the transaction. A more academic definition is provided by the Cambridge Dictionary: "a situation in which someone cannot make a fair decision because they will be affected by the result". Conflicts of interest are not limited to the financial sector. For example, they can appear in a recruitment process for a job when one of the recruiters is a friend of one of the candidates or when members of a parliament have to decide on their own remuneration. If not adequately addressed, conflicts of interest may end up in suboptimal decisions, which negative consequences will somehow arise in the long-term.

In the years before the crisis, several flagrant conflicts of interest could be observed in the financial system. The efforts to minimise the consequences derived from them were, being benevolent, reduced. Therefore, ill-practices became gradually accepted by market participants and got almost unnoticed. In the following paragraphs, three conflicts of interest, focused on credit rating agencies, investment banks and accountancy firms, are discussed.

8. The power of rating

When financial markets started to develop and the number of financial instruments available increased significantly, back to 1920s, investors could no longer adequately assess all of them. They simply could not have the time and the resources to carry out a detailed analysis of each financial product, before deciding where to put their money. As a response to this, credit rating agencies were created with the purpose of providing investors with an independent and fair assessment of the financial instruments available to them. Aiming at easing comparisons amidst different financial products, credit rating agencies established a quantitative standardised hierarchy, where best products were granted an AAA status. Under this system, the lower the quality of the financial instrument, the further was the rating into the alphabet.

In paper, the business case for credit rating agencies is clear and it worked well for many years. Nonetheless, there was always an uncomfortable question to answer: "who pays?". The two immediate alternatives are "investors pay" or "issuers pay". The first alternative is not feasible from a practical point of view, as it would imply a one-to-one relationship with each investor, which would then pay only for the rating of those products in which he is interested. Besides, such a system could leave some financial instruments unrated, as no investor would show interest in them. At the same time, it would favour the creation of a "black market" of ratings amidst investors, where many of them only pay once for the rating. The solution of "investors pay" has thus many practical drawbacks. The second alternative ("issuers pay") is the one currently in use in the financial markets. Nowadays, when a market participant wishes to issue a new financial instrument, it pays a credit rating agency for the assessment of that product.

What we find here is a showcase of conflict of interest. The issuer of the financial product has two roles in the process: examinee and payer. In these circumstances, it is very unlikely that any credit rating agency will dare to give a bad qualification to a product. What is more, there are other factors which further hamper the independence of the work of the credit rating agencies. Lack of resources to deeply analyse many thousands of financial products to be issued at the same time, consultancy activities also carried out by the credit rating agencies or close ownership relations between banks and credit rating agencies are just examples of these factors.

But credit rating agencies are far from being angelical creatures operating in a sea of monsters. In some cases, they played a decisive role, via their consultancy services, in the creation of complex financial instruments to which the highest rating (AAA) could be granted. A higher rating meant that those instruments could be easier sold to naïve (or not so naïve) investors (for example, some pension funds have a restriction to invest in products of the highest rating only), which could not be aware of all the risks embedded to them. Additionally, it has been reported that they are sometimes contacting actively issuers of financial instruments, selling their services to them and describing in detail the negative consequences that not taking their services could have for the issuance (Lewis 2010). Furthermore, the power of credit rating agencies is huge: a mention to a potential downgrade can make governments of solid countries shake with fears[20].

Most of the mortgage-backed securities which severely damaged the financial system in 2008 were granted the highest possible rating (AAA), even if they later evidenced that they did

---

[20] See, for example, these articles on the reactions following the loss of France of the highest rating AAA: "France loses AAA credit rating" (The Washington Post, 13 January 2012), "Here's Why France Lost Its AAA Rating" (Business Insider, 13 January 2012), and "France stripped of prized 'AAA' credit rating by Moody's" (The Telegraph, 19 November 2012).

not to deserve such assessment. What looked like a safe investment, sound as, among others, a US Treasury Bill, ended up bringing significant losses to its holders. Credit rating agencies defended themselves by claiming that their business is just to provide an advice, which cannot make them liable if the advice turns out to be wrong. Broadly speaking, according to their reasoning, credit rating agencies rated a security based on mortgages from the poorest people in the US as safe and sound as an US Treasury Bill, this security ends up imposing significant losses to investors, and credit rating agencies are not the ones to blame, but the investor for following its professional advice. In one word, they wash their hands in front of the investor for any misjudgement in their ratings. Certainly, there are many differences between a sound financial asset rightly rated AAA and a mortgage-based security. The inability of credit rating agencies to see these differences may be due to a profound lack of knowledge (not likely) or due to other darker reasons.

As these paragraphs have tried to show, the functioning of credit rating agencies displays several conflict of interests, which must be addressed in order to restore an optimal functioning of the financial markets. Many ideas have been put on the table to change the current functioning of the credit rating agencies, especially focusing on the system of payment and the responsibility for their ratings. Moreover, there is an ongoing initiative to reduce the role of credit rating agencies in official regulation. Unfortunately, no great solution has been found and the limited remedies implemented so far have not mitigated this conflict of interest at all.

9. Hunting fees

A second conflict of interest which contributed to the collapse of the financial markets in 2008 refers to the activities of investment banks. In summary, investment banks do not have a business model by which they earn some profit from the difference between the interest received from loans granted and the interest paid for deposits received. Most of the profits of investment banks are coming from fees generated in their various activities in the financial markets, and from gains from trading in financial markets, on their own name and on behalf of customers. Such a business model, based on fees and trading, played a decisive role in the build-up of the imbalances in the market of mortgage-based securities.

As previously outlined, the underlying rationale behind mortgage-based securities was to pack some mortgages of similar characteristics and create a security from them, which could then afterwards be sold to investors, which were ranked in different layers depending on the order of payment. As long as mortgages were paid back, investors would receive these payments. With this operation, the risk from the mortgage portfolio would be diluted from the balance sheet of banks, with the subsequent benefit in terms of regulatory capital. Transforming a mortgage loan into a security is not a simple operation; indeed one needs the expertise of investment banks for it. From each transaction, investment banks got a fee, so, in their relation with the commercial banks which had the mortgages in their balance sheet, investment banks had a clear incentive to exaggerate the benefits of the process and, at the same time, not to mention too much the risks involved (which, in fact, were not that significant for the banks generating the mortgages but for those who invested in mortgage-based securities). Basically, the more mortgages were securitised, the more fees the investment bank would be taking.

Fragile like Glass

At some point in time, this dynamic could have made that the conditions for granting a mortgage to a given household were relaxed in order to formalize the maximum number possible of them for their subsequent securitisation. It was as if the only purpose of granting mortgages were not the acquisition of a house by an individual but the income and other benefits derived from their securitisation. Furthermore, when real mortgages were not enough, financial products which replicated them where created, so that the circle of creation of mortgage-based securities could not be stopped. Investment banks did not have any incentive to stop this madness, since, indeed, they were getting substantial profits, via fees, and the losses in case something went wrong with the mortgages would not affect them at all. It was almost perfect.

However, virtuous as it looked like, some investment banks realised that something dangerous was growing around mortgage-based securities and that it could explode anytime. Ethics and morality would suggest sharing these concerns with their partners in this business (commercial banks who owned the mortgages), to make them aware of the deterioration in the quality of the mortgages and the consequences it could entail. Unfortunately, this is not what investment banks did. On the contrary, they decided to make money by betting against the collapse of the mortgage-based securities they themselves were creating. So, on the one hand, they were being part of the machinery of continuous creation of new securities, even if they had significant doubts about the performance of these securities, and, at the same time, they were betting against them (Lewis 2010)[21]. With this, investment banks got two sources of income: fees and the income from their betting.

---

[21] Trying to find a simile with other industries, it is as if a car manufacturer was on purpose selling cars with defective brakes and at the same time selling the components necessary for the reparation of the brakes at a very high price.

Much has been written about the behaviour of investment banks and the responsibility they have for the financial crisis, but, ultimately, few has changed in the way they operate. Their business model has not been substantially amended and no relevant measures have been issued to try to address this enormous conflict of interest. There have been some proposals to establish a strong separation between investment and commercial banking again (the Liikanen Report in the EU, the Volcker rule in the US and the Vickers report in the UK), which seem not to be flying far in the political arena and which, in the end, shall not affect deeply the operations of investment banks. It is worth noting that these three initiatives are, broadly speaking, proposing a return to a regime similar to that of the Glass-Steagall Act, implemented in the US in the 1930s after the Great Recession.

10. Dangerous liaisons in accounting

The last conflict of interest described in this chapter focuses on accounting. The birth of accounting takes us back to XVth century, when Italian merchants started to keep a register of their operations by using a method of double entry[22]. The method evolved over time until reaching the current International Financial Reporting Standards (IFRS) and US-GAAP (Generally Accepted Accounting Principles), the two main sets of accounting rules used nowadays in the world, which devote thousands of pages to describe how operations should be accounted for under this system of double entry.

The core objective of accounting is to provide a fair view of the assets and performance of the reporting entity[23]. However, in

---

[22] For a first introduction to history of accounting, Staubus (2003) is a very interesting start.

some circumstances, reality may be hard to swallow and reporting entities may be tempted to sweeten the way they apply accounting rules. To avoid that, before being published, financial statements of all kind of entities are subject to a detailed examination by an independent third party, the auditor. The auditor's task is mainly to ensure that accounting principles are strictly followed and that the financial statements truly reflect the situation and performance of the entity. Independence of the auditor is thus of the essence for the credibility of the information in the financial statements.

Unfortunately, auditors face a conflict of interest similar to that of credit rating agencies: they are paid by the entity they have to assess. Therefore, it would not be certainly welcomed by the reporting entity if the auditor finds many objections to the numbers presented to them. After all, it is always possible to get a different auditor in the market, which will not cause such inconveniences. Only in extreme cases, when difficulties of the entity are so evident that it is impossible to hide them anymore, auditors have raised a word of warning (for example, in the case of Bankia in May 2012). What is more, in some cases the auditing firms have a consultancy arm which helps the reporting entity to prepare their accounting statements according to their needs, what includes taking interpretations of accounting rules to the limit.

To take an example outside the banking domain, the bankruptcy of Enron, a commodity supplier in the US, is a clear example of these close links between auditing firms and audited entities. One of the main devices defined by the auditing firm, via its consultancy arm, was to create many off-balance sheet vehicles, which the accounting standards allowed to exclude from the

---

[23] In the accounting domain, "reporting entity" is the name given to the institution, financial or not, applying the accounting rules. In this section, focused on accounting, this term will mostly be used.

perimeter of consolidation, through which accounting numbers could be manipulated at will[24].

This example takes us to the third leg of this conflict of interest. Off-balance sheet vehicles were allowed by accounting standards, so in principle Enron was not doing anything illegal. The question is that auditing firms are, at least in the case of IFRS, responsible of drafting the accounting standards. The role of public authorities (regulators and supervisors included) remains minimal. Certainly, governance of the International Accounting Standards Board (IASB), the institution drafting the IFRS, has improved in the last years, but still funding and staff are mainly provided by the big auditing firms.

Basically, as summarized in Schema 2, we have a picture where auditing firms (i) are influential in the drafting of accounting rules, (ii) advice reporting entities on how to best apply accounting rules for their interests, and (iii) must audit accounting information taking the role of independent third party. Accounting firms hence control all the process of accounting and adapt it to best suit their interests (or those of their customers), not necessarily in line with those of the public at large.

---

[24] In this case, auditors could only certify the correctness of the financial statements of Enron, without touching upon any of the off-balance sheet vehicles, which were out of the scope of their work.

Fragile like Glass

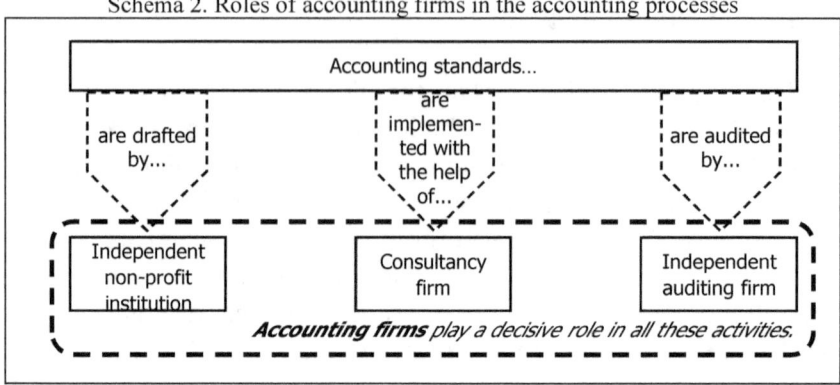

Schema 2. Roles of accounting firms in the accounting processes

In addition to that, not being directly responsible for the financial turmoil we find ourselves in now, it is clear that current accounting standards have remarkable flaws which have contributed to magnify the effects of the crisis (see Box 3).

Box 3. Accounting flaws in the crisis

Accounting rules had something to say in the financial crisis, since some of them contributed to the build-up of imbalances and to hide the real situation of the reporting entities. In this box, three areas where accounting played a major role in the unwinding of the financial crisis are described.

First, the extensive use of fair value instead of acquisition cost for the measurements of assets (and even liabilities) was behind some striking headlines in 2008 with record losses by some of the financial institutions in trouble.

Variations in fair values are reflected in the profit or loss statement of the period, as gains or losses. Acquisition costs were used in the past to value all the long-term assets of reporting entities, being a very conservative method of valuation which gave little way for gains or losses. Indeed, under this method, for example, a building acquired in 1925 would appear in the balance sheet by the value of its acquisition in 1925, regardless of potential revaluations. Fair value was first introduced for those assets held for their immediate sale, where it would make more sense to refer to the market price and not to the acquisition cost. Fair value soon started to be more attractive for reporting entities because fair value increases were recorded as gains. In comparison, acquisition cost did not lead to the recognition of any gain at all. Accounting rules evolved and soon acquisition cost became a minority method for the valuation of assets. This trend was more acute in financial institutions, since fair value was extended to most of the financial assets held in balance sheet.

Needless to say, given its positive impact, reporting entities were quick in recognising fair value gains but, as the crisis evidenced itself, they were a bit more hesitant when they had to recognize losses. In this sense, fair value is very pro-cyclical, since in the upward phase of the cycle increases significantly the profits of the reporting entities and in the downward phase, if correctly applied, imposes severe losses to them. Moreover, these gains were fictitious, since they were not supported by any real transaction; in reality they reflected the potential gains the reporting entity could obtain if the asset was sold at that point in time, but they were just potential, there was nothing substantial behind. These gains increased the net profit of the year and allowed generous dividends to be paid to shareholders, with all the implications that such action may bring. Again, the economic underlying basis of these gains was non-existent and they mainly reflected the market mood, rather than a real perception of the performance and state of the reporting entity.

In the case of those financial liabilities which were allowed to be measured at fair value (for example, bonds issued by the reporting entity), the delirious scenario was that when the fair value of these liabilities decreased due to concerns about the financial soundness of the reporting entity, a gain had to be recognized, contributing them to the presentation of a "fake" profit at the end of the period. Many banks in the last years have reported a profit as a consequence of fair value gains arising from their own liabilities[25].

Second, in the current accounting framework of IFRS and US-GAAP, when the value of an asset decreases below the amount by which it is recognized in balance sheet, an impairment loss must be charged to the income statement of the year[26]. The calculation of the current value of the asset can be carried out referring to two models: incurred losses or expected losses. In the second one, now preferred in the regulatory and supervisory community, impairment losses are recognized if the entity expects to suffer losses from it in the future; that is to say, this is a forward-looking approach. The method currently into force is the incurred loss, according to which only when a loss from the asset has materialised, the reporting entity has evidence of a decrease in its value and shall charge an impairment loss. In few words, here, the impairment regime does not anticipate future potential losses and brings the bulk of them when they are real, no longer potential. In this case, again, the model of incurred losses for impairment did not reflect the real value of the assets, since it did not consider potential declines in

---

[25] See, among others, the articles "Fair Value Accounting Haunts Banking Sector" (Wall Street Journal, 4 May 2012) or "Banks' own credit risk hampers financial results" (Risk.net, 5 August 2009).

[26] In the whole accounting domain, impairment (or provisioning) policies are a special case since it is based on potential future losses and not on gains and losses effectively incurred. Impairment only applies to assets kept at amortised cost. For those at fair value, it is understood that fair value changes will immediately reflect any potential threat to the performance of the asset.

> value. Discussions on how to implement the change from a model of incurred losses to a model of expected losses are taking very long time, with little progress so far.
>
> Lastly, the provisions in accounting rules not to include certain entities in the perimeter of consolidation also played a role in the build-up of imbalances in the years prior to the crisis. In those years, many of the riskiest business undertaken by reporting entities were transferred to these off-balance sheet entities, with which the reporting entities had, in principle, no link. As a consequence, these entities were not included in the consolidated balance sheet, which looked like pretty sound and not especially risky. When problems in the off-balance sheet entities emerged, the existence of these off-balance sheet entities came to light and reporting entities were called to rescue them, even if they had previously claimed that this would never happen. In the end, it was all a manoeuvre to reduce the risks shown in the balance sheet of the reporting entities but they had to step in when the situation started to get worse. As mentioned in the main text, these practices were recurrently followed by Enron (see Healy and Palepu 2003, Hodak 2007 and Thomas 2002 for further details).

As in the case of credit rating agencies, there is not a unique formula to solve this conflict of interest. Having said that, though, current efforts to address them are globally uncoordinated and not grasping the issue at stake. Accounting differences between Europe (IFRS) and US (US-GAAP) are still significant and little progress towards convergence has taken place, despite the continuous calls by the G20 for a more vigorous attitude of accounting-standard setters. Very few have been advanced in the enhancement of the accounting standards since 2008. Moreover, governance of standard setters is only very slowly enhanced and the conflict of interest of auditors remains nowadays outside the sight of supervisors and regulators.

Chapter 4: Capital Requirements

It is well enough that people of the nation do not understand our banking and money system, for if they did, I believe there would be a revolution before tomorrow morning.

Henry Ford

The attitude of regulators and supervisors during the building up of the imbalances which led to the financial crisis is by itself an additional factor which contributed to increase the damage caused to the financial system and to the real economy. The area where this attitude was more evident is undoubtedly the determination of capital requirements of banks. At the time when guardians should be watching closely, they seemed to be looking somewhere else or to be excessively optimistic. The following paragraphs discuss the need of capital requirements for banks at a global level, and the evolution of them in the last years in a move which severely diminished the capacity of banks to withstand losses. This happened, as seen in Chapter 2, in the framework of a more vulnerable and fragile financial system.

11. The case for regulating banks

The main business of a standard bank is to take deposits from the public and to use these funds to grant loans to customers. Depositors have the right to use their money at any time, although experience shows that they do not require all their money back at the same time. Therefore, banks can use a fairly stable proportion of these deposits to grant loans to customers, which are usually long-term. Hence the expression "maturity transformation" is recurrently used to describe the core business of banks: take short-term deposits and grant long-term loans. At this stage, under this stylized approach, the two main risks for the banks are (i) a bank run (that is to say, depositors going at the same time to the bank to retire their money) and (ii) loans not being paid back.

The first of these risks (bank runs) is currently addressed by public authorities with the establishment of Deposit Guarantee Schemes, according to which the government effectively backs up deposits up to a certain amount (100,000 € in the EU and 250,000 USD in the US). Leaving aside some unintended consequences of the introduction of Deposit Guarantee Schemes (Admati 2013), they do provide certainty to depositors that their money is safe in the bank. Reality has proven this statement true as well as false. The Spanish bank Bankia, in May 2012, is an example of a bank in difficulties which did not suffer a severe decrease in deposits, while the British Northern Rock, back to 2007, serves as example of a bank run pulling down the whole bank. After all, as Mervyn King, former Governor of Bank of England, once said, it is not rational to start a bank run but it is rational to be among the first ones in it. Actually, first "bank runners" will take their money back, probably with interest, since the troubled bank will still have assets to cover that, but late "bank runners" are left in uncertainty about when they will recover their money, despite the assurance given by Deposit Guarantee Schemes.

Furthermore, it must be noted how the use of funding sources other than deposits have created new risks of "runs" for the bank, which are no more limited to retail depositors. For example, in late 2011 European banks were confronted with a "run" from US Money Market Funds, which were concerned about the strength of

Fragile like Glass

European banks and suddenly withdraw their short-term funding. In this case, there was no queue of people in front of the bank to withdraw their money: everything happened in a more subtle way: the US Money Market Funds stopped rolling-over the very short-term funding in USD they provided to European banks[27]. At that juncture, the European Central Bank had to establish a direct swap line with the Fed in order to allow European banks to get funds in dollars.

Box 4. The fragile equilibrium between deposits and loans

In this box, we design a very stylized example to illustrate the fragility of banks when confronted with debtors in arrears (that is, not paying back the loans)[28]. The core of traditional banking transactions is to take deposits from customers and, with these funds, to grant loans to other institutions. The bank obtains its profit from the difference between the interest received from loans and the interest paid to depositors. Nonetheless, this way of operating is very fragile and depends, to a great extent, on the assumption that all loans will be paid back.

To illustrate this statement, let's assume a hypothetical bank which takes 100 deposits of 10 € from its customers, at an interest rate of 1%, and grants 100 loans of 10 € at an interest rate of 6%. Both deposits and loans have the same maturity. At the end of the maturity of the deposits and loans, the following flows are going to and leaving the bank:

---

[27] See European Systemic Risk Board (2011).
[28] The example cannot be applicable to investment banks, which activity does not involve granting loans and getting deposits from customers. Their business model is rather different and consequently they are not so heavily affected by debtors in arrears.

Deposits: 1000 € (repayment of deposits) + 10 € (interest) = 1010 €

Loans: 1000 € (repayment of loans) + 60 € (interest) = 1060 €

The profit for the bank is thus 50 €, the difference between the inflows (1060 €) and the outflows (1010 €).

Let's suppose now that 7 of the loans (7%) are not paid back at the end of the period. In such a case, the flows related to the operations of the bank are:

Deposits: 1000 € (repayment of deposits) + 10 € (interest) = 1010 €

Loans: 930 € (repayment of loans) + 55,8 € (interest of 93 loans) = 985,8 €

In this case, the bank gets 24,2 € less than the amount it must pay to its depositors.

This stylized example serves to illustrate how quick a bank can pass from generating a profit to have losses which endanger its survival. However, it simplifies too much the way banks operate nowadays.

In order to try to get closer to the real operation of banks on the liabilities side, let's assume that 10% of the deposits are held with the central bank, with no interest to be paid by the bank. In addition, let's say that the deposits and loans are constantly rolled over, so that they can be considered as stable. We continue to assume that 7% of the loans are not paid back.

In this case, the cash outflows from deposits are 9 € (interest paid to 90 deposits) whereas the cash inflows from loans are 55,8 € (interest from performing loans). In addition to this, we must count

Fragile like Glass

> on the non-performing loans, which do not pay interest to the bank and which principal (70 €) is lost.
>
> Hence, the bank experiences a loss of 23,2 € (calculated as 55,8 € - 9 € - 70 €).

The second large risk that a bank faces relates to the loans it grants. Box 4 has shown how even if a small amount of loans are not paid back, they can seriously endanger the survival of the bank. To address this problem, capital regulation was introduced globally in the 1980s via the so-called "Basel Accords". The basic principle of capital regulation is to force banks to keep a proportion of their assets (loans in our stylized example) as reserves, which they can use to compensate potential losses coming from the loans. These reserves (also called equity or capital) can be formed mainly from contributions of shareholders or from retained profits of previous years. Looking from a different angle, capital requirements imply that banks can fund with debt (namely, deposits and other loans received) only a given proportion of their loans (see Schema 3 below).

Schema 3. Minimum capital requirements in the balance sheet of a bank

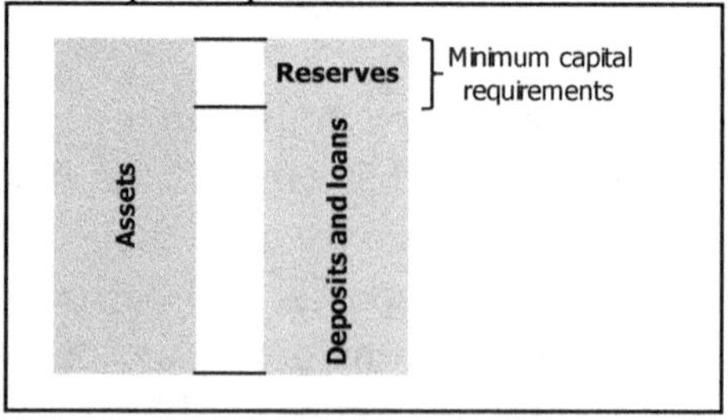

12. The evolution of capital requirements

The first version of the Basel Capital Accord (Basel I) was simple and straightforward: banks had to keep 8% of their assets as capital, weighted in a very simple scale. Soon afterwards, banks started to lobby against this rule, by stating that the one-size-fits-all solution did not consider appropriately the different risks and nature of the financial assets held by the banks. In 1994, Basel II was issued, containing two important "enhancements": (i) the expansion of risk weights, and (ii) the possibility of using own internal methods to calculate the capital requirements.

Starting by the latter, in Basel II banks were authorized to use their own internal models to calculate the capital requirements they had to maintain. The rationale behind it states that banks know better than anybody else the assets they hold and therefore are in a better position to assess their risks exposures and, ultimately, to determine their capital requirements. It can also be seen from the contrary point of view, as entrusting the fox to guard the chickens.

But even as misleading as it may seem, the introduction of internal models was minimised by the other "enhancement". The introduction of risk weights can be qualified as the largest success in the history of lobbying by banks. According to the new methodology, instead of using total assets for the calculation of the capital requirements of banks, banks can allocate different risk weights to the assets, depending on the level of risk they have. What is more, an approach of incrementing risk weights as the risk of a given asset is higher, but always keeping a floor of 1, was discarded and Basel II defined many categories of assets with a risk weight below 1 and even some of them with zero risk weight (for example, sovereign debt). A risk weight of zero implies that this asset is risk-free and can, in no way, impose any loss to the holder of it, an assumption which can be qualified as daring, at the

Fragile like Glass

minimum. Capital requirements would be then calculated from the risk weighted assets, not from the amount of total assets. Assets with zero-risk weights would then lead to no additional capital requirement: they have no cost in terms of capital for the bank.

The obvious consequence of the introduction of Basel II[29] was a reduction in the absolute level of capital as per total assets. Banks undertook important efforts to optimize the risk weights of their assets and financial instruments with low risk weights became very popular in the financial markets. From the 8% of Basel I, many banks moved to levels of capital ratios just above 2% (calculated following Basel I methodology)[30]. A level of capital of 2% means that a reduction in the value of all the assets of the bank of just 2% would dry up all the equity of the bank[31]. Nevertheless, this scary situation was pretty in line with the legal framework, as banks were keeping the levels of capital mandated by Basel II, on the basis of risk weighted assets. Basically, risk weights diminished significantly the amount of assets to compute on the denominator of the capital ratio. Several studies suggest that the average risk weight applied by banks to its financial assets is close to 55%[32]. That means that, on average, banks are holding half of the capital they should be required to if risk weights had not been introduced in Basel II.

---

[29] It must be noted that US did not introduce Basel II for all its banks as US authorities did not feel comfortable with the concept of risk weights. This did not save US banks from not being strongly capitalized when the financial crisis hit them in 2008.

[30] Basically, under Basel I the capital requirements were calculated as the ratio between equity (E) and assets (A): E/A. With the introduction of risk weights, capital requirements are calculated as the ratio between equity (E) and risk weighted assets (RW*A). If we exclude risk weights (RW) from this ratio, we have actually the definition of capital requirements in Basel I.

[31] A scenario where all the assets of the bank suffer a reduction in value at the same time is not very realistic. However, an equivalent scenario where an important portion of the assets of the bank declines in value by 10% is not so far from reality and would have the same devastating effects on the equity of the bank.

[32] See Le Leslé and Avramova (2012) for further details

Regulators and supervisors attended from a privileged position to this process of reduction in the capital requirements of the entities they were entitled to regulate and supervise. From a different angle, banks had more assets and less capital to withstand losses stemming from these assets. Needless to say, when the crisis hit, banks were found to have very little capital to withstand losses and had to knock on the door of governments to ask for public (taxpayer) support.

The recent introduction of Basel III does only partially cover some of the fundamental flaws in Basel II. Under Basel III, banks shall have a higher amount of capital, which is also defined in a stricter way to make sure that what is there is really able to withstand losses. Moreover, the introduction of the liquidity framework and of the leverage ratio (which is the capital ratio of Basel I with different name)[33] is also a major improvement in the right direction.

13. Higher capital requirements or growth

As we have seen in previous paragraphs, when the crisis hit, banks had very low levels of capital to withstand losses from their assets. The significant growth in the balance sheet of banks was not accompanied by a similar growth in capital, which, thanks to the introduction of risk weights in Basel II, actually diminished considerably in the years before the crisis. The logical response of regulators and supervisors in Basel III, when confronted with this situation, has been to increase capital requirements for banks in order to build-up enough buffers to withstand future losses.

---

[33] Basically, the capital ratio in Basel I is the ratio between equity and assets (E/A), whereas the leverage ratio compares the assets with equity (A/E). Both ratios use the same variables in the numerator and in the denominator.

Fragile like Glass

However, it must be noted that the issue with risk weights remains unaddressed.

The response from banks to these higher capital requirements has been based on the assumption that they will affect their ability to grant loans to the real economy and will, then, have negative effects on growth. In their reasoning, they argue that resources which could be otherwise lent to the real economy would need to be frozen in order to meet these higher capital requirements. In other words, banks propose here a choice between capital or loans, as both of them are not possible simultaneously.

This argumentation mixes the sources of funds of the bank with how banks allocate them to the real economy[34]. What capital requirements fix is the proportion of the funds which the bank can obtain with debt and the proportion which it must generate internally, via issuances of shares, retained earnings, or any other form. These sources of funding do not have anything to do with how the funds are tapped in the economy as loans, securities or other financial instruments. The fact that capital requirements increase does not necessarily mean that there are less loans which can be granted to the economy; it implies that less loans (or other assets) would be financed by debt. Then, higher capital requirements just impose a limitation in the level of indebtedness of the bank. Only when the bank decides to meet the higher capital requirements via a reduction of their assets, which is a decision of the bank itself, the argument that higher capital requirements will come at the cost of growth may have some justification.

To understand how this would work, let's imagine a regulatory framework with a capital requirement of 10% and a bank with 10 € of capital, 90 € of debt and 100 € of total assets[35], all of which are

---

[34] See Admati (2013) for further details.

loans to the real economy. The bank has a capital ratio of 10%, fully in line with its capital requirements. Afterwards, the regulator decides to increase the capital ratio to 12%. The bank has two options for complying with the new capital regulation, depending on whether it acts on the numerator or on the denominator of the ratio. The bank can decide to increase its capital, with, for example, an issuance of shares[36], to 12 € and to reduce its debt to 88 €, keeping thus 100 € which it can lend to the real economy[37]. In this case, capital requirements do not affect the real economy. Alternatively, the bank can pursue the 12% capital requirement from the denominator of the ratio. So, if it reduces its assets to 83 € (and its debt to 73 €) and maintains its capital in 10 €, the bank would meet the capital requirement of 12%. In this case, the bank is lending less to the real economy, as a consequence of the reduction of its assets, but this is a choice of the bank to meet the capital requirements. Schema 4 below summarizes both alternatives available to the bank.

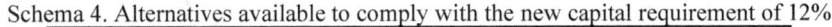
Schema 4. Alternatives available to comply with the new capital requirement of 12%

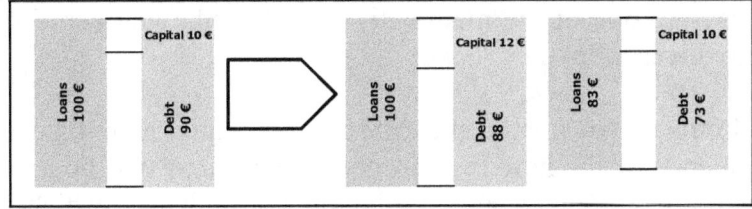

---

[35] For the sake of clarity, we do not refer to risk-weighted assets in this example. Alternatively, we could perfectly say that 100 € are the risk-weighted assets. Whichever the option taken is, it does not change significantly the results of this hypothetical example.

[36] Alternatively, the bank can decide to increase capital by retaining profits and not distributing them to shareholders via dividends.

[37] In case the bank cannot reduce its debt for whatever reasons, it should raise capital to 13 € to comply with the new capital requirement of 12%. This scenario does not substantially change the example, so it is not further considered.

Fragile like Glass

However, the second option does not automatically imply that growth is affected by it. What happens is that a given bank is not injecting 17 € of credit to the real economy, but it may be the case that, as banks theoretically operate in a competitive free market, other banks are providing this necessary credit to the economy or, even more, that the real economy does not need this credit to grow because there is an excess of credit or because the credit is financing inefficient activities. What is more, now, under the 12% capital requirement, the bank is better capitalized and prepared to withstand negative shocks which may hit it, what also brings benefits to the economy as a whole.

Furthermore, in our example above, we have assumed that all the loans are granted to the real economy, but it may be the case that banks have other kind of investments (this assumption would be closer to reality) and it reduces them, not the credit to the real economy, to meet the new capital requirement of 12%. As discussed in other sections of this book, granting loans to the real economy are one of the main activities of banks, but certainly not the only investment they make.

Moreover, if finally the size of the bank is reduced as a consequence of the new capital requirement, that will be a way to tackle the "Too-Big-To-Fail" problem of some banks, which are so large that their failure could take with them the government which tries to rescue them (for example, Ireland or Cyprus). When some banks grow so much that they can be considered, by themselves and by the market, "Too-Big-To-Fail", they have the implicit guarantee (via lower costs of borrowing, for example) that they will never fail, whatever risky activities they enter into. This implicit guarantee introduces an externality in the financial markets and clearly distorts their functioning. Hence, the reduction of the total assets of banks should not be seen as a big catastrophe for the financial system.

The statement that higher capital requirements negatively affect credit to the real economy may just be hiding the fact that the profit per share, as well as the dividend, decreases with higher capital. Broadly speaking, these higher capital requirements can be met with the reclassification of a proportion of the profit of the year, leaving thus less profit available for dividends, with a capital increase, which would imply that more shareholders shall share the same amount of profits as dividends, or with a reduction of assets, which may hamper the ability of the bank to generate the same level of profits in the future. Any of these measures would certainly not be welcomed by existing shareholders and by the high management of the bank. The recurrent reference to the credit to the real economy seems to be just an excuse to maintain current (and irreal) levels of profitability per share of banks.

Going back to our example, it may be the case that, after all, banking is not such a competitive market as it should be and that the 17 € are really lost and the real economy will not get the funding it needs to grow. The optimal reaction to this is not to give up the new capital requirement of 12 €, but to encourage competition by easing the access to the market of new banks, for example. Recent debates in Europe, though, seem to suggest a certain over-dimension of the banking sector in the EU, pointing then at the opposite direction.

To sum up, it seems that higher capital requirements may bring a wide array of benefits to the financial system, not necessarily hampering the contribution of credit to growth. To that end, it is essential to keep clear in our minds that capital requirements only affects the proportion of the bank assets which are funded with debt and with own funds (or capital), not what banks do with their assets. In our stylized example above, we have seen how an increase in capital requirements does not automatically bring negative consequences for the financial system, even if an individual bank chooses to meet it via a reduction of its assets. The reasoning used by banks seems to have as ultimate goal the desire to keep the *status quo*, where most of the assets of banks are funded with debt, which is easier to get but which introduces further risks in the financial system, and where generous dividends can be distributed. Certainly, the low levels of capital with which banks operated before the financial crisis cannot be the benchmark for the design of a safer financial system.

Chapter 5: Policy Bites

The dogmas of the quiet past are inadequate to the stormy present. The occasion is piled high with difficulty, and we must rise with the occasion. As our case is new, so we must think anew and act anew.

2nd State of the Union address (1862), Abraham Lincoln

In previous chapters, we have tried to describe the main factors which have shaped the financial system as it stands now, including the unraveling of the financial crisis itself. These chapters have a clear descriptive character. In these pages, we will try to answer the question of whether the proposals for reform of the financial system are going in the right direction or whether, on the contrary, they are aimed at a wrong target. In other words, we leave the descriptive world and move into the realm of policy. In the previous section, we have already hinted at the effect of higher capital requirements for banks, as one of the most immediate measures proposed, and in the coming paragraphs we will go further into some other fields which the reform of the financial system could touch upon.

14. Does it need to be so complex?

In the last years, financial markets have significantly grown in complexity and the largest banks have become probably the most complex institutions in the world. Most of them are active in a significant number of countries and currencies, in many different

Fragile like Glass

business areas and in the vanguard of financial innovation. Following this trend, the Basel Capital Accords have also increased in complexity. For example, using a rough but powerful indicator of complexity, the document establishing the Basel I framework has only 26 pages, Basel II is defined in a document of 347 pages and Basel III final documentation will probably go beyond 1,000 pages.

In general terms, this increase in complexity in the Basel Capital Accords has been generally understood as the necessary price to pay for the increase in complexity in the financial system. Nonetheless, some regulators (Haldane 2012, and Hoenig 2012 and 2013) have recently raised their voice against this growing complexity. In their view, the current financial system is too complex and banks have become black boxes, even for themselves. Simple rules (such as the leverage ratio or the ratio of non-deposit liabilities to GDP) can help to shed light into these dark boxes and market discipline will consequently act to correct potential imbalances. In the end, it is not necessary to have detailed knowledge of the pipes of the banks, but just to use some very basic indicators which can be reliably used by supervisors, regulators and the public at large.

Furthermore, it is desirable to have a simpler framework for the supervision, which shall be based in easy principles and shall not contain many exemptions or special treatment for some transactions. While most of the banking regulation is originally born as a single principle, the number of exceptions and special cases which are subsequently added (thanks, mostly, to the action of lobbying groups), multiply the complexity and hamper the initial objective of the regulation. Many valuable resources of supervisors are currently devoted to checking compliance of banks with complex regulations and the introduction of simpler regulations could free these resources, which could then carry out deeper analysis of the institutions under supervision. In this sense, in many cases supervision has become a mere tick-the-box activity, given the complexity and extension of financial regulation in force.

To put it simple, against the statement that complex entities need complex regulations, a new trend is growing stating that complex entities can and should have simple regulation.

One way for assessing whether simple rules serve to regulate complex entities is to look at other fields for similar cases. In this case, we can find, at least, the following two relevant cases:

- Speed limits. Speed limits in our roads are unique, regardless of the kind of car we are driving. There are no different limits for new cars, for older cars, for Ferraris, for Fiat, for yellow cars, for cars with one passenger or based on any other feature of the car. There is a single limit and few excuses. In this sense, speed limits are a perfect example of "one-size-fits-all". The only exceptions are trucks and buses, given their considerable size and the negative consequences which driving too fast could have, in what could be considered a simile for the SIFI buffer[38]. Furthermore, the strict limits in the amount of alcohol in blood when driving, a policy which makes sense due to the risks derived from this practice, draws many parallelisms with certain financial products, which use could be restricted or even not be allowed. Rather than going to a system with multiple limits tailored to each kind of vehicle, which could end up with millions of speed limits depending on the characteristics of the car and of the

---

[38] Under Basel III, those banks labeled as Systemically Important Financial Institutions (SIFI), after the assessment carried out according to the criteria made public by the Basel Committee on Banking Supervision, are subject to higher capital requirements via a SIFI buffer. Needless to say, no bank in the world is claiming to be a SIFI.

driver, a single speed limit allows easy implementation and supervision by the traffic police[39] . It is true that a Ferrari can drive faster than a Fiat and that a speed limit does not consider the "particular specifications" of the Ferrari, but this seem to be the price to pay for a workable organisation of our roads.

- Personal income taxes. Personal income taxes are designed to charge the income obtained by individuals during the year, applying different methods depending on the source of the income: work, investments in real estate, rental payments, dividends, investments in financial markets, economic activities as sole proprietors, inheritance,... In this case, the number of different sources of income which the tax authorities can find is infinite. Tax authorities are confronted with the challenge of defining a simplified and enforceable system which is able to capture all the potential cases which can generate an income for an individual and, at the same time, does not give rise to unnecessary complexity which for 99% of the individuals is irrelevant. With different levels of success, the regulation of income taxes in developed countries, although complex and obscure in some certain areas, seems to tend towards further simplification (OECD 2012).

These are just two examples of how complexity of financial regulation must not be the necessary result of the increasing complexity of operations in the financial markets. Our traffic systems and taxation are two fields confronted with important complexity in their functioning and, nonetheless, they have come up with a simplified version for their control. The introduction of

---

[39] Otherwise, imagine the hard work of police officers in speed traps trying to define the characteristics of the car and the speed limit applicable to it.

simpler rules for banks could have the important benefit of easing the tasks of supervisors, which are now facing a complex regulation which puts them in a situation of disadvantage vis-à-vis their supervised entities.

It is clear that the other extreme, summarized by the principle of "the one-size-fits-all", is neither a desirable outcome, but the optimal solution seems to be closer to it than to "tailored regulation", which comes at the price of excessive complexity. Ultimately, the greatest beneficiaries from complexity in financial regulation are those able to allocate significant resources in finding loopholes and grey areas in the legal provisions which can benefit them.

15. Liquidity and solvency: chicken and egg

When regulators have expressed their views in favour of stricter capital requirements, one of the most recurrent answers by banks and their lobbying groups has been to define this crisis as a liquidity crisis, not as a solvency crisis. Consequently, according to this view, what is needed to solve the crisis is the injection of further liquidity into the system. Under the same line of argumentation, introducing stricter capital requirements will drain liquidity from the system, exacerbating the effects of the crisis.

Before entering into the discussion of the current crisis, let's have a look first at the issue from a theoretical point of view. Here, it has been widely evidenced that concerns about the solvency of a bank will always damage its liquidity, whereas the opposite chain of events (liquidity concerns provoking a solvency crisis) do not always hold. The mechanism for solvency concerns to negatively affect liquidity is rather straightforward. In a stylized way, when other institutions start to suspect of the weak solvency state of a given institution, they increase their requirements (via higher spreads, increased collateral guarantees or simply refusing operations with it) to enter any transaction with them. These higher costs have an immediate effect on the liquidity of the institution under solvency problems, which, at the same time, have more problems finding the necessary liquid funds to honor existing commitments. The case of liquidity concerns hampering the solvency of an institution is less evident. For example, temporary liquidity problems of a sound institution may be solved easily, since that institution will always find willing counterparties in the financial markets. A different case is defined by liquidity problems of an institution with an unsustainable model, a problem which, sooner or later, will be reflected in its solvency.

It is clear now that the events of the autumn of 2008 froze financial markets and halted the normal course of financial transactions in them. As a consequence of that, many positions remained open and foreseen sources of liquidity were no longer available. To help banks to manage their most immediate treasury needs, central banks worldwide opened direct credit lines, agreed to have swap facilities in different currencies and, with a longer-term perspective, allowed banks to take liquidity from them at a very low cost. Even more, in 2012, at the height of the EU sovereign crisis, the European Central Bank pumped 1 trillion € to the banks, in very favourable conditions, to be returned in three years. These actions seem to reflect the important liquidity implications of the crisis and the clear compromise of authorities to return to a normal situation. Consequently, liquidity was made available for those with temporary liquidity problems. At the same time, the limited effect of these injections of liquidity in containing the negative consequences of the crisis also highlights that something else must be done in other areas.

On the other hand, it can also be argued that the crisis itself was not triggered by a lack of liquidity, but by negative returns of risky investments (mortgage-based securities, to be more precise) and a weak position of financial institutions to compensate the losses generated by them. In 2008, the financial system was in a very fragile equilibrium and a blow-wind from a corner in the market (mortgage-based securities) had tremendous effects on them. If financial institutions had been just amidst liquidity difficulties but sound in terms of solvency, they should have easily found counterparties in the financial markets. This was true for those institutions which were estimated by the markets to be sounder (for example, as they had a wide depositor base, guarantees by their government or a solid capital position). The fact that some institutions have survived the crisis and some others not (for example, Bear Stearns or Dexia) should not have been possible if the crisis had just been a liquidity crisis, since all of them were experiencing the same difficulties when markets froze and all of them had the same access to the liquidity provided by central banks. Ultimately, it was the solvency position of each one of them which determined how they emerged after the crisis: some were perceived as weak and no liquidity was available to them anymore, whereas some others could fulfil their liquidity requirements, with more or less problems, depending on how easily other participants in financial markets were eager to trade with them. Certainly, for some institutions, there are liquidity constraints, but these cannot be solved with the injection of more liquid funds to them, since what must be corrected is their solvency position or their business model. Injecting liquidity without taking care of solvency would be the equivalent of providing a painkiller to a sick person but without going to the source of his sickness.

Therefore, pumping more liquidity to the financial system as it stands now will not improve the health of financial institutions in the long-term and will most likely only have the effect of artificially keeping inefficient ("zombie") banks alive. Additionally, it can create a bubble in some markets, as financial institutions will use these funds to generate quick returns to them, with which compensate losses from other areas and, at the same time, strengthen their capital position. The evidence from the behaviour of financial markets in the last years suggest that an excess of liquidity will likely give rise to a bubble somewhere; financial bubbles are becoming more frequent now: dotcom bubble, real-estate bubbles in US, UK, Ireland and Spain, bubble in emerging countries, bubble in commodities and gold,...

To conclude, massive injections of cheap liquidity cannot be the only solution to the crisis, since they are most likely going to generate further problems in the medium-term (via bubbles in some markets) and they do not address the source of the concerns in financial markets. It is necessary to build a regime where resilience of the banks, in terms of solvency, is strengthened and where inefficient banks can be closed down without imposing significant costs to the public and without disrupting the normal course of business in the real economy.

16.   Purveyors of credit to the real economy

As already discussed, the main activity of banks consist of taking deposits from the public and with these funds grant loans to customers, in order to fund their investment projects[40]. With the term "customers", it is understood that non-financial corporations and households (the real economy) are the main beneficiaries of these loans, which would imply a welfare improvement for society,

---

[40] Actually, in the US, non-financial corporations have easier access to financial markets than in Europe. For the purposes of this section, we will assume that the situation is equivalent in both jurisdictions.

via the better living conditions of the households, via the loans directly or the income generated by non-financial corporations. Thus, banks are at the cockpit of real economy, ensuring that a sufficient amount of funds is made available for achieving new projects and investments. An economy without a sufficient provision of credit to the real economy is certain to decline in the medium- and long-term.

Banks, bankers and lobbying groups use this argument against any regulatory effort undertaken since the crisis, in order to scare regulators and supervisors of the consequences that any tightening of the regulation would have for the real economy, and in a call to get a preferential treatment from the public sector in case of trouble. In the case of new regulation, according to this way of thinking, if the regulators and supervisors try to tighten it, such actions would immediately prevent banks for granting loans to the real economy and innocent households and non-financial corporations would suffer the consequences of the daring new regulation.

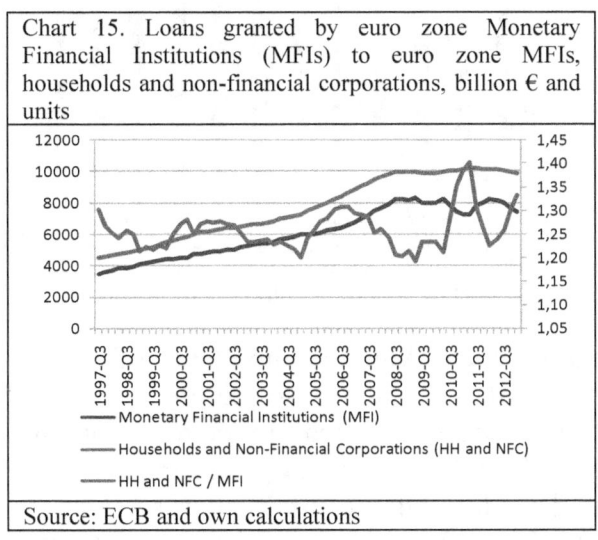

Chart 15. Loans granted by euro zone Monetary Financial Institutions (MFIs) to euro zone MFIs, households and non-financial corporations, billion € and units

Source: ECB and own calculations

Fragile like Glass

First of all, let's see whether banks do really grant so many loans to the real economy as they claim. A look at the loans granted by banks in the euro zone to households and non-financial corporations, in comparison to the loans granted to other banks (MFIs in the ECB terminology), for example, shows that they have followed similar and parallel trends since 1997 (see Chart 15). At least in the euro zone, banks are granting slightly more loans to the real economy than to other banks. Indeed, the distribution of loans between banks and the real economy has remained, at least for the euro zone, stable over time (with values between 1,20 and 1,35), despite such significant events as the introduction of the euro or new regulatory regimes like Basel II.

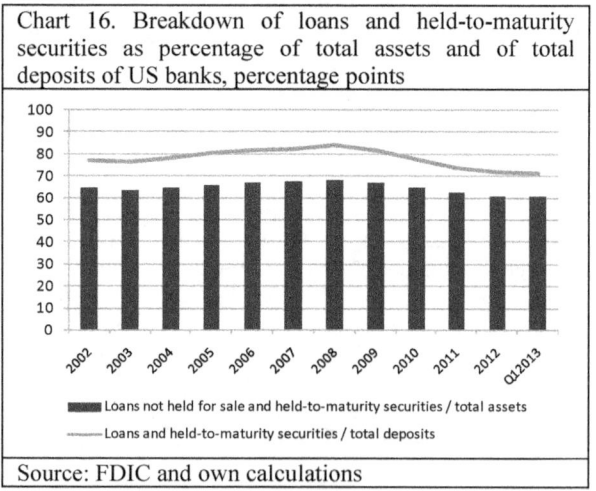

Chart 16. Breakdown of loans and held-to-maturity securities as percentage of total assets and of total deposits of US banks, percentage points

Source: FDIC and own calculations

It is also worth checking the importance of the loans and held-to-maturity securities, assumed to be the assets more directly related with the provision of credit to the real economy, in the total balance sheet of banks in the last years. In this case, the lack of comparable data for Europe limits the sample to US banks. According to Chart 16, loans and held-to-maturity investments (whichever the counterparty, banks or the real economy) have remain stable between 60% and 70% of the total assets in the last ten years. The introduction of the Dodd-Frank Act in 2010 apparently had little effect on the decisions of the banks.

Looking at the relation of loans and held-to-maturity securities with the total deposits, it can be observed how they have declined significantly since 2008, following an increase in previous years. This fall is, though, not caused by a reduction on the assets side (loans), but stemming from an increase in deposits. In this case, thus, core deposits have been more volatile throughout the crisis than the provision of credit to the real economy, which remains over time as the main activity of banks.

As already discussed in Box 4, granting loans to bad customers can have dramatic consequences for the bank. Thus, granting loans per se cannot be the policy objective of banks, and regulators and supervisors should take actions to prevent that credit is granted in a way that it endangers the survival of the bank. That is to say, the provision of credit to the real economy should happen at the request of the real economy (demand side), never implying that there should be a constant amount of credit to it from the supply side. In an ideal financial system, if some project in the real economy needs credit and it is viable, it will certainly find some bank to finance it, regardless of the financial regulation in place.

Therefore, financial regulation which encourages (or promotes) larger volumes of lending to the real economy, pushing from the supply side, would inevitably end up financing activities and transactions which do not make sense from an economic point of view (for example, several airports in the middle of nowhere in Spain). Such actions will, sooner or later, create a credit bubble, with disastrous consequences for the real economy it tried to protect. Thus, this line of argumentation used by banks may turn

Fragile like Glass

out to be quite negative in the long-term. What is more, it cannot justify keeping them with an undue level of capital.

Similarly, the fact that a bank is providing credit to the real economy should not automatically imply that the public authorities shall protect it from insolvency, to the point of almost being impossible for a bank to default. The concerns of public authorities in the event of the default of a bank should indeed be on the protection of depositors, not on where the defaulting bank invested the money from the deposits. If the banking system is free and open for competence, the space left by any insolvent bank would soon be filled by competitors or, even better in terms of competence, by new banks. Unfortunately, the banking system seems to have followed an opposite path, with increased concentration and important barriers to the entry of new competitors.

Thus, to use the provision of credit to the real economy from a supply side, just for the sake of it, to justify a privileged treatment in terms of capital requirements or insolvency is not justified, as it seems not to respect the core economic principles of free competence, and formation of prices from supply and demand.

17. The (not so) almighty monetary policy

Monetary policy is at the heart of the activities of central banks, which through the regulation of the amount of money into circulation, seek to maintain a certain variation in prices (inflation) which does not damage the acquisition power of the society. To that purpose, central banks have three main tools: interest rates, exchange rates[41] and operations with banks (which include reserve

---

[41] The effects of variations in exchange rates on inflation are indirect and are provoked by an increase or decrease in the demand of exported or imported goods and

requirements, deposits and credit facilities, and any other transaction with them).

Following the end of the second oil crisis, back to 1981, monetary policy started to develop towards a model where central bank independence was granted and where a fixed objective in terms of inflation rate was defined by law. Nowhere is this trend clearest observed as in the creation of the European Central Bank, which has an inflation target of close to 2% and which forced all governments in the euro area to pass laws granting the independence of its central bank. Such an approach had the main goal of isolating monetary policy from politics, which could no longer use it for its own benefits at the cost of higher inflation rates for the future. Monetary policy worked efficiently at that time as inflation rates were steadily in low levels, when compared with two-digit inflation levels in the 70s.

As already indicated above, in order to implement their decisions on monetary policy in practice, central banks are constantly working on the side of money supply, entering into periodic transactions with banks under their jurisdiction. The amounts involved in the transactions of the ECB and of the Fed (central banks of the euro area and of the USA, respectively) have been growing in the last years, as evidenced by Chart 17 below. Actually, the ECB entered into more transactions than the Fed between 1998 and 2008, but when the financial crisis erupted, the Fed reacted promptly and significantly increased the monetary base. Since then, while the Fed has continued with this increase in the monetary base, the ECB has reduced its lending to euro area financial institutions twice, once in 2011 and also in 2013. Between

---

services. The most immediate effects of such a policy are first felt in the real economy. In the last years, the free floating of currencies has diminished the capacity of a central bank to use exchange rates as a tool. For the sake of comprehensiveness, exchange rates have been enumerated as a tool for monetary policy, although rarely used nowadays, with the notable exception of the Swiss Central Bank.

Fragile like Glass

2011 and 2012 the recourse to the ECB increased more than threefold. There has been more volatility in the amounts lent to euro area banks than in the equivalent variable in the US during the crisis.

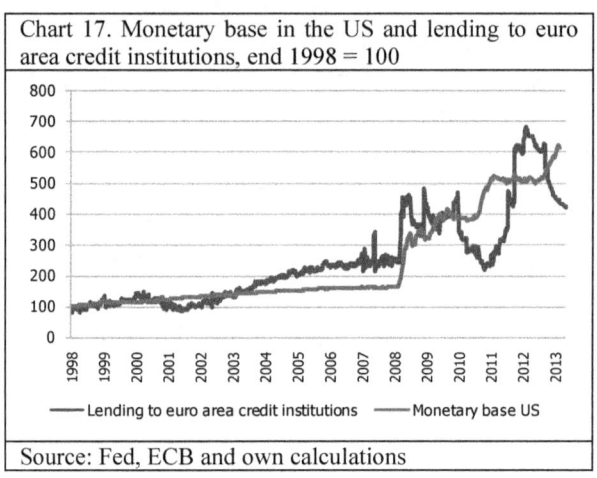

Chart 17. Monetary base in the US and lending to euro area credit institutions, end 1998 = 100

Source: Fed, ECB and own calculations

Through the operations with banks, central banks have been pumping significant amounts of liquidity to the financial system. Together with it, the creation of money in bank intermediation also increased the amount of money available in both areas. Chart 18 below shows the evolution of the monetary aggregates M2 and M3 in the US and the euro zone[42], respectively. It can be seen how the aggregates have been since the first observation always with positive growth rates, with peaks beyond 10% in both cases[43].

So, be it from operations with central banks or be it from the process of bank intermediation, the financial system got higher

---

[42] In 2006, The Fed decided not to publish any more its time series of M3, so M2 had to be used in Chart 18.
[43] The significant deceleration of the growth of M3 in the euro area between November 2007 and April 2010 surely deserves a very detailed and deep analysis, which, unfortunately, is out of the scope of this book.

amounts of money on a continuous basis in the last years. Consequently, banks were in the need of allocating these funds to any activity. They could place them as deposits in the central bank and get a low return or, alternatively, they could invest them with the expectation of a higher return. Following the second option, some banks decided to extend mortgages to not-very-sound households or to lend the money again within the financial system (mainly to other banks abroad). In other cases, banks decided to design a complex array of financial products which could generate some profits in the short-term and which would be hedged against undesired events by using other new financial products (derivatives) which compensated the behaviour of the first ones.

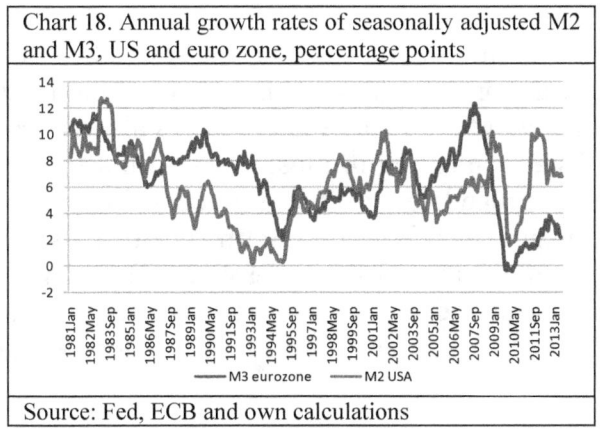

Chart 18. Annual growth rates of seasonally adjusted M2 and M3, US and euro zone, percentage points

Source: Fed, ECB and own calculations

Therefore, a significant proportion of this money never reached the real economy, as it was intended to do. This fact could be due to the lack of demand of credit from the real economy: if nobody was entering the bank asking for a loan, the bank had to find another use to give to this money. In other words, the underlying issue is, as hinted in another sections of this text, whether the demand of credit can grow continuously over time (following the rhythm of the money available in the financial markets) or whether it has already reached its maximum level. If the former, banks could have easily channeled the money they were getting from the operations with central banks to the real economy. Unfortunately, this was not the case (see Charts 15 and 16). It can also be possible that although there was a demand from the real economy banks decided to embark into more profitable transactions or that they even did not find any other use to give to the money, since the demand of credit by the real economy remained stable. For whatever reason, bottom line is that there was an excess of liquidity in the financial system, which was not pumping it into the real economy. This excess had to be somehow given a profitable use, putting pressure on banks to find new innovative ways to be able to generate profits from it.

Returning to the role of monetary policy in this process, it did not only have a word to say at the inception of the financial crisis. Its role as the main tool to solve the crisis is also under discussion. Central banks are entrusted in most cases with a financial stability and supervisory mandate, so they are active institutions in acting against the negative effects of the financial crisis. Nonetheless, most of the monetary policy measures to counterweight the negative effects of the crisis, significant in amounts as Chart 17 discloses, have had so far limited effects, for several different reasons.

First, financial markets have become global and banks are highly interconnected, so the scope of the measures taken by one central bank in isolation in the whole world is also limited. At the current stage, it is very difficult for monetary policy to significantly affect the behaviour of large cross-border banks unless it is coordinated among the major economies in the world (namely, US, Europe and Japan), which may be in a different phase of the cycle or which may have a different agenda. Moreover, monetary policy as it is conducted now, was founded under a different scenario, that after the Second World War. The assumptions and the models which worked well for the past fifty years are no longer valid, since, as already described in Chapter 2, financial markets have dramatically changed in the last ten years. This change has also hampered the grounds on which monetary policy is based.

What is more, the financial system has changed so much in the last years that there may never be a "return to normal". The current scenario, where we have been in the last five or six years, may become the normal scenario in the future. In this case, monetary policy will not be able to do much in favour of financial stability, and new and more direct ways and tools to affect the behaviour of banks shall be explored by supervisors and regulators. Monetary policy will undoubtedly continue to be decisive in the determination of the inflation rate, but it will be forced to work together with the financial stability and the supervisory domains in order not to create unintended consequences from its decisions. Although powerful, monetary policy does not seem to be able to revert alone the effect of the crisis, a task which seems to be now shared with supervisors and regulators.

18. Regulators and supervisors reloaded

In Chapter 4, we have discussed the several steps taken in the development of capital requirements worldwide and we have noted how new releases of the Basel Accord have resulted in lower levels of capital (if calculated without risk weights) and with increasing complexity. In addition to that, regulators and supervisors in most cases were not able to address the growing imbalances on time and, in some other, they even showed some myopia as they did not take action until the very last moment. Since 2008, many voices have asked for a re-organisation of the institutions in charge of financial regulation and supervision, given their apparent inability to prevent the formation of imbalances which led to the current financial crisis.

Before assessing the different proposals put on the table, it is important to look at the possible motivations of the behaviour of regulators and supervisors in the build-up of the financial crisis. Actually, there are many factors which can explain why they did not manage to see the elephant in the room.

First, there is a clear imbalance in the resources available in banks and those which the supervisors have. It has to be borne in mind that supervisory authorities do not have more than 2,000 employees at maximum, and they often must supervise entities with thousands of employees and a wide array of activities worldwide. What is more, in terms of compensation, supervisory authorities cannot compete with banks. In this scenario, supervisors are confronted with an increasingly complex regulation and with an environment where cross-border activities, which require due coordination with other supervisors, are more important, absorbing most of their time and leaving few resources for carrying out effective supervision as such. Therefore, supervisors are always one step behind the banks, be it in the search for loopholes in the regulation, in the development of any new products or in the economic assessment of the consequences of new practices in the financial markets.

Second, the free movement of capital flows has turned the world into a gigantic market for financial services, where the country of residence of the bank is not an insurmountable obstacle for offering products and services in the other corner of the world. Competition has become fierce worldwide and many countries have strong political interests in ensuring that their largest banks ("national champions") do not lose this fight. Supervisors are hence afraid of curtailing the ability of their local banks to compete globally and, obviously, banks are often using arguments in this direction, against any tightening of financial regulation[44]. Therefore, capturing their regulators and supervisors with these arguments, "national champions" started a race-to-the-bottom in capital requirements and a sky-is-the-limit attitude towards risk taking. Interactions between lobbying groups and supervisors started to be more frequent and the clear line which should exist between supervisors and supervised entities became blurred. The recent discussions in the European Union and the weird positions taken by some Member States regarding the implementation of the Basel III Accord, via the so-called CRD IV, seem to be a good example of this phenomenon.

Related with the former, "supervisory capture" can also explain the behaviour of supervisors during the building-up of imbalances in the years prior to 2008. "Supervisory capture" exists when the supervisor falls under the influence of the entity it has to supervise and it no longer has the ultimate power to impose its criteria over the supervised entity. "Supervisory capture" is often related to the own organisational functioning of supervisors and how the incentives of individuals in it are aligned or, better said, misaligned with the overall social objective of supervision. The concept of "supervisory capture" comprises many practices, ranging from the personal relations between supervisors and staff of the supervised entity to revolving doors policies and career concerns. For example, it has been widely observed that many supervisors move to the entities they supervise after some years, and a very tough assessment of a bank by a supervisor could prevent this movement from happening. In the same line, nobody wants to raise problems to the managers and supervisors are not an exception, so they tend to minimize the number of issues raised

---

[44] To name just the three most recurrent, banks arguments usually refer to the level playing field, to the relocation of services to other countries or to the businesses lost in favour of competitors.

upwards during the supervisory process. In other cases, it was the political sphere which urged supervisors not to raise many concerns regarding the situation of banks.

Actually, probably as a combination of these three and of other factors, there were not many dissenting voices in the regulatory community in those years (see Rajan 2005, for a notorious exception) and there seemed to be a widespread self-fulfilling confidence in the resilience of the system, which can be summarized by the quote from Alan Greenspan: "We had been lulled into a state of complacency". In this case, regulators and supervisors were somehow absorbed by the optimism in the financial market and they did not have the courage to stop the music when the party was at its peak.

Concerning the organisational structure of supervision, whether it should be organised in one single entity or under a "twin-peaks" model, the crisis has shown that supervisors in both cases. Much was written before the crisis about the optimal organisational design of supervision and the crisis seems to have solved the issue by itself, as countries with an almighty supervisory authority as well as countries with separated independent supervisory agencies have seen their banks deep into difficulties. Hindsight has shown that the debate was, policy speaking, superfluous.

The debate on the best way to carry out regulation and supervision of banks should not focus on the institutional domain, since the institutional design ultimately depends on many factors, such as the history of the institutions of the country, the choices of neighbouring countries or the size of the financial sector. What is essential is that the supervisory and regulatory authorities have enough resources to make them fully and truly independent from the political sector, on the one hand, and from the banking sector, on the other. Granting this independence, would make regulators and supervisors strong against the claims from the public sector or from the banking sector to relax their requirements. In addition to that, of course, an effective system of regulation and supervision shall adequately address the three points highlighted above (broadly speaking, resources, defence of "national champions" and supervisory capture).

In the last years, the debate has shifted from a discussion on the institutional design to an investigation on the most effective way to define macro- and micro-prudential supervisory responsibilities[45]. It is clear that both aspects of supervision are interrelated but it is also clear that they pursue different objectives. Metaphorically, one could say that macro-prudential supervision cares about the health of the forest as a whole whereas micro-prudential supervision looks at the health of each individual tree in the forest. Together with the challenges outlined in the previous paragraph, it is important that a balanced relation between both areas of supervision exists, in order not to give too much prominence to one at the expense of the other.

19. Fewer names in the banking system

One of the, probably unintended, consequences of the crisis has been the increase in concentration in the banking system. During the days following the fall of Lehman Brothers, many troubled banks were "invited" to be acquired by sounder banks, increasing the size of existing banks and reducing its number. This was just the latest chapter of a process which started back in the 1980s and which has seen the number of banks significantly reduced. Since 2000, this phenomenon of concentration has been

---

[45] For example, Masciandaro (2009) and IMF (2013). For a comprehensive discussion on the contents of micro- and macro-prudential supervision, see Borio (2003).

Fragile like Glass

more acute. This trend has also been complemented by the fact that no new banks have entered the financial system, where the traditional names remain.

An obvious consequence of this concentration is the decrease in competition and the threat that the banking system becomes an oligopoly, with negative implications for the society in terms of costs of the services offered. It is clear that it is easier to reach an oligopolistic agreement within a group of twenty than when there are hundreds of counterparts. Nonetheless, the existence of oligopolistic practises is very difficult to proof in court, although the recent scandal on the fixation of the LIBOR interest rates (see Box 5) provides a clear example that such agreements may exist in reality.

Box 5. The LIBOR scandal

The London Interbank Offered Rate (LIBOR) is one of the main interest rates used in transactions in the financial markets. It is set by a pool of banks, which submitted the interest rates they expected to charge in their operations in different currencies and maturities (quotes). The LIBOR is the most widely used reference interest rate in the financial markets. References in contracts like "LIBOR + 30 basis points" are rather common.

From an investigation in the trading activities of Barclays, it emerged that the bank had contacted other banks in the pool of the LIBOR to agree on the quotes to report in order not to hamper their trading activities of a given day. Although initially denied, it was later known that this was usual practice among all the banks participating in the pool and that highest management was also aware of that. Actually, US authorities found out that that Barclays was submitting fake low quotes in 2008 to avoid getting the attention of the supervisors for being in difficulties. Back to those days, an entity posting high quotes for their funding would be considered as having troubles finding new funds and would then be given special attention and probably acquired by the government. By posting fake quotes, Barclays gave the impression that its business was strong and not much affected by the developments in financial markets at that time.

After these events were known by the public, there was a strong call for a reform of the system. The issue is nonetheless not easy to solve. The first immediate reaction was that several banks left the pool of LIBOR since they perceived an increased reputational risk if stricter governance was imposed on them. This movement, if widespread, could hamper the coverage of the LIBOR itself. Even more, many have proposed to use interest rates in real transactions, but this would imply very important implementation costs and would introduce a backward character to the LIBOR, whereas it has always had a certain forward nature. It would always be possible to use only a sample of real transactions, but this would have the negative effect of losing representativeness. The most logic reaction to tackle this issue places itself in a significant increase in governance, probably moving supervision of the LIBOR quotes to a supervisory authority.

What is more difficult to address is the issue that several banks agree to provide fake quotes to preserve he profit of some operations of them. A logical reaction to this would be to increase the pool of banks as much as possible, but already the contrary is happening: there are less banks reporting to the LIBOR pool. Actually, this scandal has shown that the possibility of banks acting as oligopolies is real and regulators and supervisors should promptly devote special attention to detect and correct these practices.

Fragile like Glass

Another effect of concentration in the banking system is the increase in size of banks, which can be more powerful than their home countries. Banks are becoming often larger than the economies of their countries, measured by the Gross Domestic Product (GDP)[46], and have the potential to substantially damage the economic growth of countries (see Charts 19 and 20). Indeed, Ireland, Spain and Cyprus have experienced severe budgetary difficulties stemming from the support provided to their falling banking system. The problem also exists in the US, despite the size of its economy and its developed financial markets.

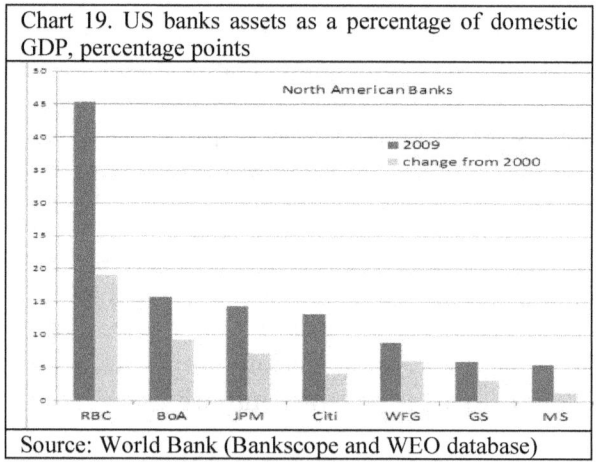

Chart 19. US banks assets as a percentage of domestic GDP, percentage points

Source: World Bank (Bankscope and WEO database)

In this context, banks know that they are able to bring down a country and they use this power to ensure that their survival is not

---

[46] Despite its wide use as a proxy of the size of the economy of a country, the use of the Gross Domestic Product (GDP) raises some methodological concerns. To mention just the main one, these charts compare the level of a variable (total assets) in one moment in time (end of the accounting year) with a variable (GDP) which covers a period of time (a year). Actually, GDP measures the added value of the goods and services produced by a country during a year, it does only indirectly measures the economic activity during the year and even more indirectly the size of an economy. Nonetheless, on the other hand, GDP is widely used as reference variable in this kind of analysis and it is very easily understood by readers.

under threat: they are "Too-Big-To-Fail". In this case, as the collapse of these huge banking groups would have devastating consequences for the economy of the home country, the probability of such an event happening comes closer to zero. In other words, when banks are in difficulties, it is almost certain that the government will intervene to save them, in order to avoid the effects which the collapse of such a big player would have. Therefore, banks enjoy a kind of subsidy, usually in the form of lower financing costs; since, ultimately, the public sector is guaranteeing their assets. For example, non-financial corporations do not have such an implicit guarantee. From a certain point of view, the increase in size of banks has made them immortal.

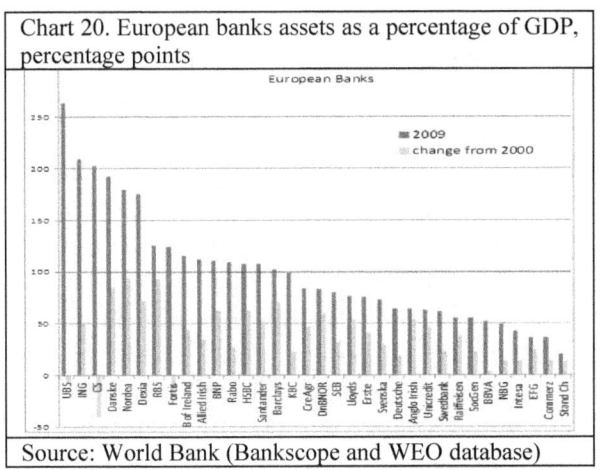

Chart 20. European banks assets as a percentage of GDP, percentage points

Source: World Bank (Bankscope and WEO database)

What can be done then to reverse this dangerous trend? There are mainly two areas where to focus.

The first one is the introduction of a powerful and clear resolution regime, covering even the more complex banks. The presumption that a big bank in severe difficulties cannot be closed down must be removed. Therefore, it is necessary to define a strong resolution regime, which states very clearly the different steps to be

Fragile like Glass

taken in case of trouble and the institution in charge of them. To avoid potential political interferences, the resolution authority in charge of the process should be independent from the public sector and have strong incentives to act promptly. On the side of banks, it is important that they are required to prepare realistic and enforceable "living wills", which define how supervisors and regulators should act when the bank enters into difficulties. Living wills shall ensure that the bank is cut into pieces, with the essential activities (for example, retail deposits) being kept, but with the troubled ones being dismantled. Needless to say, the obstacles raised by banks in this process are quite significant, since they see this as a real threat to their current favorable status.

The second area of work for regulators and supervisors in addressing the issue of "Too-Big-To-Fail" must be the reduction of the size of the main banks and the entrance of new banks into the market. Nothing can be made at this stage in order to reduce the current size of banks but further attention should be devoted by authorities of competence on the dangers that a concentration of the banking system may bring to the public. At the same time, the entrance of new banks should be encouraged, since the requirements to initiate banking activities in a given country are quite harsh at the present moment. Nonetheless, in general, national supervisors and regulators are not comfortable with the entrance of foreign competitors and try to protect their banking system. Whether this is a wise solution or not remains to be seen, but it is at least contrary to the free movement of capitals which govern most of the Western economies.

A more radical idea, to be further investigated, to tackle the increasing concentration in the banking system would be to limit the maximum market share which banks (or any other financial institution) can enjoy. Here, it would be the competence (or anti-trust) authorities those acting. The case of Standard Oil Corporation in the 1920s and how US authorities split the company into seven provides a good example of how a similar policy worked.

20. Fields of data warehouses

It has been argued that the imbalances which led to the financial crisis could not be adequately detected with the information available to supervisors and regulators at that time. In other words, available data did not alert of what was coming. Under this line of argumentation, to avoid this to happen again, there is a need to increase the amount of information collected for supervisory purposes. Accordingly, the more information is in the hands of regulators and supervisors, the better.

Such an approach must be considered with care, since the fact that more information is made available to supervisors and regulators does not automatically means that better decisions are taken (see Haldane 2013b). Indeed, there is a limit in the amount of information which a human brain can process and over-flooding the decision-making bodies of supervisors and regulators with a myriad of charts and tables may only have the effect of creating confusion and of hampering the process of decision making. At a certain point in decision-making processes, more data only introduces noise in the process and thus becomes counterproductive.

The presumption that there was not available information to identify the imbalances before the crisis can also be rebutted[47]. In those countries which experienced a bubble in the real estate sector (Ireland, United States and Spain, just to name three), there were public time series which showed a significant increase in the price

---

[47] Indeed, throughout this text I have used information already available in Internet to build the different charts which support the text in some sections. See the Bibliography for further details about these sources of data.

of housing, in the volume of credit from banks to the real estate sector and in the effort of households to acquire a house. In the case of Greece, it was clear from available data that their public sector was not sustainable. The same is valid for the excessive growth of the banking systems of some countries (for example, Cyprus) or for the increase in trading strategies in financial markets. Instead of saying that the necessary information to identify these phenomena was not available, one could say that the attention of supervisors and regulators was focused somewhere else, but not on some simple indicators available to them.

What is more, it shall always be borne in mind that information has also a cost to be produced and it must be carefully assessed whether the benefits derived from it can outweigh these costs. The fact that there are computers and IT systems able to work with tremendous amounts of data shall not immediately imply that they must be used for the collection of massive amounts of information. In this vein, for example, it seems that collecting information on a security-by-security basis has little value for regulators and supervisors, which need to prepare gigantic IT systems to manage these important flows of information and which must further aggregate if any use is to be made of it. What is more, data quality issues may hamper the use of the information for analytical purposes, keeping it just stored but not ready to use. In the end, this calls to the question of which is the purpose of collecting information if it cannot be used. From this angle, it is worse having information which cannot be used than not to having relevant information[48].

---

[48] See the recent debate in the US about the collection of information by the SEC from quoted entities using complex IT systems, while not using it for the analysis. The article "U.S. House panel probes SEC's use of outdated technology" (Reuters, 10 September 2013) provides a good summary of the issue.

It is true that there were probably areas which need better information, as they were hidden from the scope of supervisory information (see FSB and IMF 2009). Financial markets have evolved significantly in the last years and, unfortunately, the field of financial information did not always moved forward at the same pace. Nonetheless, these needs have to be fulfilled with care and they cannot lead to a process where information is required just for the sake of having it "just in case" or because it is "nice to have". In the end, having too much information about each tree in the forest can make that we lose sight of the tree and of the forest as a whole, destroying any process of decision-making to be based on such information.

In some cases, it seems that reporting requirements have lost connection with the real needs of decision-makers, which should be the ultimately driver of the information submitted to regulators and supervisors. In the area of information, size does not matters the most, but also quality and timeliness. In financial markets which evolve in a matter of seconds, more focus of financial information should be on timeliness and not on content. That is to say, rather than expanding the amount of information which must be reported on a quarterly (or half-annual) basis with a minimum delay of at least six weeks (in other words, information which is six weeks outdated)[49], the focus should be placed on having access to real-time basic information from the financial markets and from the main institutions operating in them. Although not easy, IT infrastructures allow for this process to happen.

Otherwise, decisions will be taken relying on detailed information which is too old, a fact which can make that the final

---

[49] Such information is certainly useful to determine trends and shifts in the financial system. When put in relation with macroeconomic data, this information defines the structure of the economy as a whole. It is of the essence that it remains available but it shall be used wisely and efficiently (in other words, that all information collected is used and not simply stored).

Fragile like Glass

decision taken is not the optimal under the market circumstances of that time.

Chapter 6: Of Incentives and Values

Call it what you will, incentives are what get people to work harder.

Nikita Khrushchev

The discussion held so far has been placed at the level of the institutions, focusing on abstract entities such as "banks" and not entering into the human beings behind each decision of the institution. This final section changes slightly this approach and considers mainly the people taking decisions in the institutions. After all, a bank itself does not decide anything; they are those running it, with their own system of incentives and values, who do.

To that end, following usual practice in economics, human beings are assumed to be fully rationale in their decision-making processes. As we will see, this small movement away from abstract concepts and "back down to Earth" draws interesting conclusions and must be read in complement to the more "institution-centric" approach in previous sections of this text.

21. The stick, the carrot and rational decisions

Throughout this text, we have gone through the determinants of the financial crisis, which exploded in 2008 as the combination of many different factors. We have also discussed several special features of banks and some of the policy options currently being proposed to address the situation in the financial markets. The

Fragile like Glass

focus of previous sections has therefore laid on the institutional aspect of the financial system, leaving outside the analysis the fact that banks, regulators, supervisors and other participating institutions are composed by many human beings, which react in a rationale way to the incentives they are given.

In several passages, we have briefly touched upon the role of incentives. Among others, one can highlight the following:

- Bank managers were given clear incentives to increase immediate profits when their variable compensation was linked to the annual profit of the bank.
- When stock markets started to pay to some market participants per trade entered with them, they were given a strong incentive to trade for the sake of it.
- If supervisors know that they can get a well remunerated position in a bank under their scrutiny in a few years time, they are given a large incentive not to carry out a strict supervision, in order not to hamper their envisaged movement.
- Rating agencies are paid by the issuer of the security they are rating, so they have a clear incentive to meet the expectations of the issuer in terms of rating, because otherwise they will be replaced by a competitor willing to adapt more to the customer.

These examples show us the power that incentives have in defining policy for the financial system. After all, banks are composed by individuals, who act rationally and who respond rationally to the given incentives. Providing them with incentives to do the wrong thing may have negative consequences for the system, so it is of the utmost importance to define policies which produce no negative unintended incentives. Otherwise, the effectiveness of a policy measure would be weakened by new vulnerabilities or threats arising from it. The same is valid for supervisors and regulators, which may fall sometimes under the so-called "supervisory capture", as discussed in previous sections.

When considering incentives in policy making, it must also borne in mind the ultimate objective of the institutions affected by the decision and how the decision may interfere with this. Sometimes, this task is really obvious. For example, it may simply involve considering that banks want to maximise the dividends they pay to shareholders when defining a policy which calls for retention of profits and increase of capital. In some cases, complexity and interconnectedness in the financial system make this a difficult and titanic task. A good example is provided by the margin requirements for derivative transactions not cleared in Central Counterparties (CCPs)[50], where a number of conflicting objectives interplay. Among others, the following can be mentioned: banks aiming at reducing the cost in terms of capital requirements of the new margins, non-banks operating with derivatives aiming at designing strict margin requirements for banks as a way to increase their business, Central Counterparties aiming at discouraging trading outside their venues as they would otherwise lose market share, or non-financial corporations looking for a simple and cheap way of hedging some of their operations. As we can see, this is an area with an array of conflicting interests, where special care must be paid in finding a right balance among them.

---

[50] Very broadly and without entering into many details, in the derivative transactions, outside and within a CCP, members shall post a certain amount of collateral, depending on their soundness, in order to back up the transactions in case they fail to honor their commitment. Margin requirements are a way of addressing this issue, as the collateral requirements are defined as an additional amount to that included in the transaction (a margin).

Fragile like Glass

Applying a policy which does not balance all the interest runs the risk of creating new vulnerabilities which, sooner or later, will need to be addressed by regulators and supervisors. The policy may work for a time but its unintended consequences will come to light at a certain point in time. For example, the introduction of zero risk weights for sovereign debt exposures in Basel II may explain the increase in the holdings of sovereign debt observed in some European banking systems since 2010. Actually, excessive holdings of sovereign debt in troubled European countries have recently been a matter of concern for European regulators and supervisors.

Furthermore, incentives can also be used by regulators to affect the behaviour of banks. Here, they are a powerful tool to be used in the design of policies for the financial system. Incentives play the role of the carrot in the typical cartoon showing us a horse running desperately after a carrot which the rider of the horse keeps flying in front of him. For example, under the new version of the Capital Requirements Directive (CRD) in the EU, which translates the Basel III Accord to the EU, exposures to Small and Medium-Sized Entities (SMEs) are given a lower risk weight, in an attempt by the regulator to encourage lending to SMEs, against other forms of lending which are apparently not so much linked to the real economy. However, it is not sure whether this incentive does not goes too far and promotes excessive lending to SMEs which would otherwise not be viable in economic terms.

Ultimately, the behaviour of banks and those ruling them (bankers) during the crisis cannot be the only result of their evil nature. Such an assumption is simplistic and completely ignores the power of incentives. Banks and bankers were only reacting to the incentives they were given, in a search for the fulfillment of their objectives. Bankers, like everyone else, pursued some objectives and acted accordingly. For example, if high capital requirements were preventing them from posting more profits via entering into more transactions financed with debt, then they directed their efforts to get capital requirements reduced. In conjunction with this rational behaviour, it was the reaction of supervisors and regulators to these demands what enabled banks to meet their objectives in the field of capital requirements. It was not something bankers achieved quickly, but over several decades. What is more, the greed showed by bankers in the last years and their obsession with quick and easy profits is just a reflection of the values of our society. Next (and last) section discusses this in more depth.

22. I want it all, I want it now

In the previous section, we have described the role that incentives play in the behaviour of banks and other institutions relevant for the financial markets. At the end of the analysis, we have mentioned the fact that bankers just responded to the incentives given to them and that their behaviour was fully rational, from an economic point of view.

What is more, bankers are just products of our society, they are not educated separately from most of us and they have not been under the influence of any external force which may have misguided their behaviour. The ambition, the greed and the lack of moral scruples they have evidenced in some passages of the financial crisis stem from values which are also present everywhere in our Western society. Unless our society is able to reject behaviours where extreme greed and unethical behaviours are tolerated, we, as society, will not succeed in building a financial system which is sound and which serves the society at large. Under this scenario, the current discussions where regulators, supervisors and banks fight fiercely, for example, for bargaining a percentage point in the capital requirement will not change anything. These bargaining may be temporarily won by regulators and supervisors but it will be followed soon by a new one, and that second one by a third one and so on and so forth. Beyond temporary measures to adjust, for a time, the behaviour of banks, it is necessary to address this issue from the root, from the values currently dominating our society. Actually, the system of values in the Western society as it was at the end of Second World War and our current system of values has shifted towards one where the individual an its immediate success are at the core.

The notion of success is certainly quite difficult to measure. Ideally, the success of a man should be measured by what he is and not by what he has. It should also cover all the areas of our lives, from the professional to the personal domains. The need to have immediate success has introduced strong pressure on us to demonstrate to the others that we are successful in terms of material goods, especially in the professional domain. Hence, ambition and search for power have risen in importance in our system of values, focusing on the individual and leaving the community behind.

Capitalism is based on hard work and equal opportunities for each member of the society to achieve its objectives. Nonetheless, in the last years the value of hard work as a natural way to success has been seriously eroded by a tendency, born in the growing role of ambition outlined in the previous paragraph, to seek quick and easy profits, often leaving behind ethical concerns. For example, moving far from the financial system, participants in reality shows like "Big Brother" are becoming idols for teenagers, occupying sometimes the place of other more solid examples they should have to form them as adults. This pattern is also reflected in the behaviour of the financial system and of those willing to use it to be get rich at any cost and as soon as possible, putting little emphasis on hard work or on ethical issues. Many of the so-called "gurus" of the financial system are only successful men and women, whose behaviour is, to put it mildly, borderline with fraud and crime, as courts are slowly demonstrating[51].

Even more, there is a strong push from the financial markets and from stakeholders to have ever-growing profits, and a scenario where profits remain stable around a given level over years is deemed to be unsatisfactory. In short, every year must be better than the previous one. However, this is not only happening in the financial system. Our capitalist economy seems to be based on ever-growing rates of whatever (sales, production or profits), where companies are forced to produce more and more, leading the economy to a situation where there is not enough demand for the products, even with the titanic efforts of marketing departments, which try to persuade us to buy something we do not need at all[52]. This fierce competition is not sustainable and may explain some predatory behaviours observed in the last years, but not only in the financial system. This phenomenon, let me insist on that, is not confined within the financial system.

Our society has thus shifted values (big ambition, lack of ethics and everlasting growth rates) and the behaviour of those running banks, confronted with wrong incentives, is just a mere reflection of this change. It is pointless to fight for percentage points in capital requirements if the issue is not addressed looking at the system of values reigning in our society. The wild years of capitalism where everything was allowed in the path to success must become a past and overcome trend, if we really have the intention to leave behind the current crisis and to make a safer financial system.

---

[51] Bernard Madoff and the Ponzi scheme he developed in his investment society and the activities with OTC derivatives of the JP Morgan office in London (known as the "London whale") provide just two recent examples of this.

[52] Bottled water and planned obsolescence are just two examples of that.

Fragile like Glass

There is a need to go back to the time where a different set of values were in place, where the pressure to be successful and perfect was not so intense, and where ethics always imposed a limit on what an individual could do in the pursue of its objectives. Otherwise, we are doomed to find workable solutions for the short-term but to have recurrent and frequent crisis, like the one we are currently immersed in.

Bibliography

Acemoglu, D and J. Robinson (2012). Why Nations Fail: the Origins of Power, Prosperity and Poverty. Crown Books, New York.

Ackermann, J (2009). Smaller banks will not make us safer. Opinion article in the Financial Times. Available at http://www.ft.com/intl/cms/s/0/9aef3d00-7c6d-11de-a7bf-00144feabdc0.html#axzz2cgReLNio

Admati, A and M. Hellwig (2013). The Bankers' New Clothes: What's Wrong with Banking and What to Do about It. Princeton University Press. Princeton, New Jersey

Afonso, A. and Ricardo M. Sousa (2009). The macroeconomic effects of fiscal policy. Working Series Paper no 991. European Central Bank. Available at http://www.ecb.int/pub/pdf/scpwps/ecbwp991.pdf

Allen, F (2008). Understanding Financial Crisis. The Wharton Global Alumni Forum. Available at http://finance.wharton.upenn.edu/~allenf/download/Vita/UnderstandingFinancialCrises-HCMC-31May08.pdf

Avi-Yonah, R (2005). The Three Goals of Taxation. Available at http://ssrn.com/abstract=796776

Basel Committee on Banking Supervision, BCBS (2013). Global systemically important banks: updated assessment methodology and the higher loss absorbency requirement. Available at http://www.bis.org/publ/bcbs255.pdf

Basel Committee on Banking Supervision, BCBS (2011). Basel III: A global regulatory framework for more resilient banks and banking systems – revised version June 2011. Bank for International Settlements. Available at http://www.bis.org/publ/bcbs189.pdf

Basel Committee on Banking Supervision, BCBS (2006). International Convergence of Capital Measurement and Capital Standards: A Revised Framework - Comprehensive Version. Bank for International Settlements. Available at http://www.bis.org/publ/bcbs128.pdf

Basel Committee on Banking Supervision, BCBS (1998). International Convergence of Capital Measurement and Capital Standards. Bank for International Settlements. Available at http://www.bis.org/publ/bcbsc111.pdf

Fragile like Glass

Borio, C (2003). Towards a macro-prudential framework for financial supervision and regulation? BIS Working Papers No 128, February

Boyer, P and J. Ponce (2011). Regulatory capture and banking supervision reform. Available at http://www.bvrie.gub.uy/local/File/JAE/2011/t_ponce_jorge_2011_%5B1%5D.pdf

Byrne, J et al (2013). The Occupy Handbook. Back Bay Books. New York

CFTC and SEC (2010). Findings Regarding the Market Events of May 6, 2010. Report of the Staffs of the CFTC and the SECT to the Joint Advisory Committee on Emerging Regulatory Issues. Available at http://www.sec.gov/news/studies/2010/marketevents-report.pdf

Collander, D, H. Fölmer et al (2009). The Financial Crisis and the Systemic Failure of Economics Academics. Working Paper 1489. Kiel Institute for World Economy. Available at http://www.ifw-members.ifw-kiel.de/publications/the-financial-crisis-and-the-systemic-failure-of-academic-economics/KWP_1489_ColanderetalFinancial%20Crisis.pdf

Congress of the United States of America (2010).Dodd-Frank Wall Street Reform and Consumer Protection Act. Available at http://www.sec.gov/about/laws/wallstreetreform-cpa.pdf

Dewatripont, M, I. Jewitt and J. Tirole (1999). The economics of career concerns, part II: Application to missions and accountability of government agencies. Review of Economic Studies 66 (1), 199-217. Available at http://citeseerx.ist.psu.edu/viewdoc/download?doi=10.1.1.147.7273&rep=rep1&type=pdf

Eichengreen, B (2005). Sterling's Past, Dollar's Future: Historical Perspectives on Reserve Currency Competition. NBER Working Paper 11336. Available at http://www.nber.org/papers/w11336

Ernst & Young (2012). US GAAP versus IFRS: The basics. Available at http://www.ey.com/Publication/vwLUAssets/US_GAAP_versus_IFRS:_The_basics_November_2012/$FILE/US_GAAP_v_IFRS_The_Basics_Nov2012.pdf

European Banking Federation (2013). EBF response to the European Commission consultation on reforming the structure of the EU banking sector. Available at http://www.ebf-fbe.eu/uploads/EBF%20response%20to%20Commission%20consultation%20paper%20on%20reforming%20the%20structure%20%20%20.pdf

European Banking Federation (2011). EBF Position on Systemic Risk. Available at http://www.ebf-fbe.eu/uploads/documents/positions/BankingReg/17%20June%202011-Position%20on%20Systemic%20Risk%20v5%20clean%20version.pdf

European Central Bank (2012). Financial Stability Review. December 2012. Available at http://www.ecb.europa.eu/pub/pdf/other/financialstabilityreview201212en.pdf

European Commission (2008). Commission Regulation (EC) No 1126/2008 of 3 November 2008 adopting certain international accounting standards in accordance with Regulation (EC) No 1606/2002 of the European Parliament and of the Council. Available at http://eur-lex.europa.eu/LexUriServ/LexUriServ.do?uri=OJ:L:2008:320:0001:0481:EN:PDF

European Securities and Markets Authority (ESMA) and European Banking Authority (EBA) (2013). ESMA-EBA Principles for Benchmark-Setting Processes in the EU. Available at http://www.esma.europa.eu/system/files/2013-658_esma-eba_principles_for_benchmark-setting_processes_in_the_eu_-_final_report.pdf

European Systemic Risk Board (2011). Recommendation of the ESRB of 22 December 2011 on US dollar denominated funding of credit institutions. Available at http://www.esrb.europa.eu/pub/pdf/recommendations/2011/ESRB_2011_2.en.pdf

Federal Reserve Bank of New York (2012). New York Fed Responds to Congressional Request for Information on Barclays - LIBOR Matter. Available at http://www.newyorkfed.org/newsevents/news/markets/2012/Barclays_LIBOR_Matter.html

Ferguson, C (2012). Inside Job: The Financiers Who Pulled Off the Heist of the Century. Oneworld Classics. London

Financial Stability Board and International Monetary Fund (2009). The Financial Crisis and Information Gaps. Available at http://www.imf.org/external/np/g20/pdf/102909.pdf

Galati, G and P. Wooldridge (2008). The Euro as a Reserve Currency: a Challenge to the Pre-Eminence of the US Dollar? International Journal of

Finance & Economics, Volume 14, Issue 1, Int. J. Fin. Econ. 14: 1–23 (2009)

Glavan, S (2010). Fair Value Accounting in Banks and the Recent Financial Crisis. Revista de Estabilidad Financiera del Banco de España, Number 19. Available at http://www.bde.es/f/webbde/Secciones/Publicaciones/InformesBoletinesRevistas/RevistaEstabilidadFinanciera/10/Nov/Fic/ref0419.pdf

Haldane, A (2013a). Constraining discretion in bank regulation. Speech given at the Federal Reserve Bank of Atlanta Conference on 'Maintaining Financial Stability: Holding a Tiger by the Tail(s)', Federal Reserve Bank of Atlanta. Available at http://www.bankofengland.co.uk/publications/Documents/speeches/2013/speech657.pdf

Haldane, A (2013b). Why institutions matter (more than ever). Speech given at the Centre for Research on Socio-Cultural Change Annual Conference, School of Oriental and African Studies, London. Available at http://www.bankofengland.co.uk/publications/Documents/speeches/2013/speech676.pdf

Haldane, A (2011). The race to zero. Speech given at the International Economic Association Sixteenth World Congress, Beijing, China. Available at http://www.bankofengland.co.uk/publications/Documents/speeches/2011/speech509.pdf

Haldane, A and V. Madouros (2012). The dog and the Frisbee. Given at the Federal Reserve Bank of Kansas City's 36th economic policy symposium, "The Changing Policy Landscape", Jackson Hole, Wyoming. Available at http://www.bankofengland.co.uk/publications/Documents/speeches/2012/speech596.pdf

Hau, H, S. Langfield and D. Marqués Ibáñez (2012). Bank ratings: what determines their quality? Working Paper Series no 1484. European Central Bank. Available at http://www.ecb.europa.eu/pub/pdf/scpwps/ecbwp1484.pdf

Healy, P and K. Palepu (2003). The Fall of Enron. Journal of Economic Perspectives, Volume 17, Number 2, Spring 2003, pp 3–26. Available at http://pubs.aeaweb.org/doi/pdfplus/10.1257/089533003765888403

High-level Expert Group on reforming the structure of the EU banking sector (2012). Final report. Available at http://ec.europa.eu/internal_market/bank/docs/high-level_expert_group/report_en.pdf

HM Treasury (2012). The Wheatley Review of LIBOR: final report. Available at https://www.gov.uk/government/uploads/system/uploads/attachment_data/file/191762/wheatley_review_libor_finalreport_280912.pdf

Hodak, M (2007). The Enron Scandal (slides). Available at http://ssrn.com/abstract=991044

Hoenig, T (2013a). Basel III Capital: A Well-Intended Illusion, Remarks by FDIC Vice Chairman Thomas M. Hoenig to the International Association of Deposit Insurers 2013 Research Conference in Basel, Switzerland. Available at http://www.fdic.gov/news/news/speeches/spapr0913.html

Hoenig, T (2013b). Safe banks need not mean slow economic growth. Opinion article in the Financial Times. Available at http://www.ft.com/intl/cms/s/0/64803c76-fe03-11e2-8785-00144feabdc0.html#axzz2cbarbJl9

Hoenig, T (2012). Back to Basics: A Better Alternative to Basel Capital Rules, delivered to The American Banker Regulatory Symposium; Washington, D.C. Available at http://www.fdic.gov/news/news/speeches/archives/2012/spsep1412_2.html

Independent Commission on Banking (2011). Final Report – Recommendations. Available at http://www.ecgi.org/documents/icb_final_report_12sep2011.pdf

Institute of International Finance (2012). Specific Impacts of Regulatory Change on End-Users, Initial Report. Available at http://www.iif.com/press/press+386.php

International Monetary Fund (2013). Key Aspects of Macroprudential Policy. Available at http://www.imf.org/external/np/pp/eng/2013/061013b.pdf

International Monetary Fund (2012). The Liberalization and Management of Capital Flows: an Institutional View. Available at http://www.imf.org/external/np/pp/eng/2012/111412.pdf

Kirilenko, A, A. Kyle, M. Samadi and T. Tuzun (2011). The Flash Crash: The Impact of High Frequency Trading on an Electronic Market. Available at http://ssrn.com/abstract=1686004

Krugman, P, and M. Obstfeld (2006). International Economics: Theory and Policy. 7th Edition. Pearson Education. New Jersey

Laux, C and C. Leuz (2010). Did Fair-Value Accounting Contribute to the Financial Crisis?. Journal of Economic Perspectives, American Economic Association, vol. 24(1), pages 93-118, Winter. Available at http://www.nber.org/papers/w15515.pdf?new_window=1

Lewis, M (2010). The big short: Inside the Doomsday Machine. W. W. Norton & Company. New York

Le Leslé, V and S. Avramova (2012). Revisiting Risk-Weighted Assets: Why Do RWAs Differ Across Countries and What Can Be Done About It? IMF Working Paper 12/90. Available at http://www.imf.org/external/pubs/ft/wp/2012/wp1290.pdf

Maslow, A.H. (1943). A Theory of Human Motivation. Psychological Review, 50(4), 370–96. Available at http://psychclassics.yorku.ca/Maslow/motivation.htm

Masciandaro, D and M. Quintyn (2009). Regulating the Regulators: the Changing Face of Financial Supervision Architectures Before and After the Crisis. Available at http://dev3.cepr.org/meets/wkcn/1/1724/papers/masciandarofinal.pdf

McGee, R (1997). Taxation and Public Finance: A Philosophical and Ethical Approach. Commentaries on the Law of Accounting & Finance, Volume 1, pp. 157-240. Available at http://dx.doi.org/10.2139/ssrn.461340

Organisation for Economic Co-Operation and Development, OECD (2012).Special Feature: Trends in personal income tax and employee social security contribution schedules. Available at http://www.oecd.org/ctp/tax-policy/50131824.pdf

Patterson, S (2012). Dark pools: The Rise of A.I. Trading Machines and the Looming Threat to Wall Street. Random House. London

Price Waterhouse Coopers (2012). IFRS and US GAAP: similarities and differences. Available at http://www.pwc.com/en_US/us/issues/ifrs-reporting/publications/assets/ifrs-and-us-gaap-similarities-and-differences-2012.pdf

Rajan, R (2005). Has Financial Development Made the World Riskier? Available at http://www.kansascityfed.org/publicat/sympos/2005/pdf/rajan2005.pdf

Romer, D (2001). Advanced Macroeconomics. McGraw-Hill. New York.

Sikula, M (2011). Crisis and Post-Crisis Adjustment and New Challenges for the Economic Science. Economic Review. Number 40, 2/2011. Available at http://www.euba.sk/veda-a-vyskum/utvary-riadene-prorektorkou-pre-vedu-a-doktorandske-studium/ekonomicke-rozhlady/aktualny-rocnik/preview-file/er2_2011_Sikula-9517.pdf

Staubus, G (2003). Accounting, Accountability, Auditing, and Financial Scandals Over the Centuries. Available at http://ssrn.com/abstract=1733229

Tarullo, D (2012). Financial Stability Regulation - Remarks at the University of Pennsylvania Law School. Available at http://www.federalreserve.gov/newsevents/speech/tarullo20121010a.pdf

Thomas, W (2002). The Rise and Fall of Enron. Available at http://leeds-faculty.colorado.edu/durhamg/fnce3010/enron.pdf

Viñals, J, J. Fiechter et al. (2010). The Making of Good Supervision: Learning to Say "No". IMF Staff Position Note SPN/10/08. Available at http://www.imf.org/external/pubs/ft/spn/2010/spn1008.pdf

Data sources

All the data shown in the Charts throughout the text have been obtained from databases held by a number of public international authorities. The following links refer to the entry page of these databases.

Banco de España: http://www.bde.es/bde/es/secciones/informes/boletines/Boletin_Estadist/ano_actual/ and http://www.bde.es/bde/es/secciones/informes/Publicaciones_an/Cuentas_Financie/anoactual/.

Bank for International Settlements: http://stats.bis.org/bis-stats-tool/org.bis.stats.ui.StatsApplication/StatsApplication.html.

European Central Bank: http://sdw.ecb.europa.eu/.

Federal Deposit Insurance Corporation: https://cdr.ffiec.gov/public/.

Federal Reserve: http://www.federalreserve.gov/econresdata/default.htm.

New York Stock Exchange: http://www.nyxdata.com/.

www.ingramcontent.com/pod-product-compliance
Lightning Source LLC
Chambersburg PA
CBHW072210170526
45158CB00002BA/525